T0067428

MINDFUL PARENT, CONSCIOUS CHILD

Venus Montgomery

BALBOA.
PRESS
A DIVISION OF HAY HOUSE

Copyright © 2017 Venus Montgomery.

All rights reserved. No part of this book may be used or reproduced by any means, graphic, electronic, or mechanical, including photocopying, recording, taping or by any information storage retrieval system without the written permission of the author except in the case of brief quotations embodied in critical articles and reviews.

Balboa Press books may be ordered through booksellers or by contacting:

Balboa Press
A Division of Hay House
1663 Liberty Drive
Bloomington, IN 47403
www.balboapress.com
1 (877) 407-4847

Because of the dynamic nature of the Internet, any web addresses or links contained in this book may have changed since publication and may no longer be valid. The views expressed in this work are solely those of the author and do not necessarily reflect the views of the publisher, and the publisher hereby disclaims any responsibility for them.

The author of this book does not dispense medical advice or prescribe the use of any technique as a form of treatment for physical, emotional, or medical problems without the advice of a physician, either directly or indirectly. The intent of the author is only to offer information of a general nature to help you in your quest for emotional and spiritual well-being. In the event you use any of the information in this book for yourself, which is your constitutional right, the author and the publisher assume no responsibility for your actions.

Any people depicted in stock imagery provided by Thinkstock are models, and such images are being used for illustrative purposes only. Certain stock imagery © Thinkstock.

Print information available on the last page.

ISBN: 978-1-5043-6080-7 (sc)
ISBN: 978-1-5043-6101-9 (e)

Balboa Press rev. date: 02/06/2017

Table of Contents

"Your children are not your children.

They are sons and daughters of Life's longing for itself.

They come through you but not from you.

And though they are with you yet they belong not to you.

You may give them your love but not your thoughts.

For they have their own thoughts.

You may house their bodies but not their souls

For their souls dwell in the house of tomorrow, which you cannot visit, not even in your dreams

You may strive to be like them, but seek not to make them like you

For life goes not backward nor tarries with yesterday

You are bows from which your children as living arrows are sent forth

The archer sees the make upon the path of the infinite, and He bends you with his might that His arrows may go swift and far

Let your bending in the archer's hand be for gladness

For even as He loves the arrow that flies, so He also loves the bow that is stable"

-Kahil Gibran

Introduction

This is a time of enlightenment, a time of awakening. We are living in a vastly different era than any of our ancestors; we're more connected yet isolated in ways they could've never imagined. Just as technology has drastically changed the way we communicate and has connected the world into a global community, we as parents need to adjust and change our way of parenting. The world we live in has changed dramatically, there often seems to be so much hatred and unrest in the external world we live in. Yet everyone seems to point the finger at the other person. As Mahatma Gandhi stated "Be the change you wish to see in the world." My friends the change we wish to see in the world begins with us, right here, right now. It begins at home with our children. Our parents and grandparents, fathers and forefathers had a recipe for childrearing that many of us continue to subscribe to. My question to you is this, if what we were taught was effective and worked, why is the world in the state it is in? Why is there so much violence in the world? It is my belief that the violence begins at home. We must all share in the responsibility if we are to make a change in the world we live in.

We have a spiritual obligation to allow our children to evolve into the spiritual beings they are meant to be and to live from their core. In order to accomplish this we must first remember that our children already possess a deeper knowing of where they came from and who they are. We must create a path to foster that innate joy and passion they are born with. We are guiding these extraordinary beings of light, our children to grow into the fullness of who they are. I will outline principles for consciously connecting with our children.

Children are people too, it may seem like a strange concept to some. It's something I feel that needs to be addressed because more often than not I hear the sentiment, that children are basically the property of the adults in charge of them. This idea couldn't be farther from the truth.

Our children are only children for a short while of their lives so while adults may believe this is my property I do what I want, that's not the case. Especially when you consider that eventually many of our children will in turn be our lawmakers, change agents and caretakers. Imagine that they will treat you as they have been treated growing up. You may want to shift your perspective and approach to how you are interacting with them. A Course in Miracles says that every action we take is either toward love or fear. Think about how a child feels when they are motivated to produce a behavior because they fear the consequences versus guiding your child through love and connection.

Many parents find it beneficial to parent from the fear based approach however, I am advocating that we instead parent from a loving and more conscious approach. There seems to be a subconscious concept that to be kind and gentle with our children is a sign of weakness. Being kind to our children is a sign of love, patience, understanding and inner strength.

In history we can easily see that ruling others through fear hasn't worked. Yet when it comes to our little ones, it seems like the go-to method.

The dictionary defines fear as a distressing emotion aroused by impending anger, danger, evil, pain. Whether the threat is real or imagined the feeling or condition of being afraid. Do we really want to raise children who constantly feel anger, pain or danger from us? I ask you, what kind of an adult comes from a fear based upbringing. One who is afraid to question anything, fearful of being their true selves, and scared to try new things.

Love on the other hand in terms of the definition used in the dictionary means a profoundly tender passionate affection for another person, a feeling of warm personal attachment.

In our society there is violence in our schools, children toting guns to school, children bullying other children, shooting their caretakers and not to mention all the violence against children. All of this is a wakeup call that there is a drastic change needed in the world today.

It is my hope that something I say resonates with you a cocreating conscious parent.

In the end, no matter the method of raising our children, it is ultimately their choice in who they become. Will there be lots of mistakes, if they are lucky-yes there will be many mistakes made and opportunities to learn and grow from. Will there be experiences in life that we never saw coming, of course but just like a quote I saw on Instagram the other day says "to the spiritual man both good and bad experiences are like his left and right hand . . . he uses both"

I am a parent on this extraordinary path of self-discovery while also assisting this being of light (my son) to know who he is and to remember his true nature. I believe we all have unique talents and gifts that we can share with each other to enrich our souls.

It is my intention to open up this dialogue and begin to parent not from what society tells us but from the inside out. I hope that this book will lead to much collaboration in the future with other parents who hold the same vision for our children and together we can co-create whole beings.

This book is to share my journey with you. I am sharing what works for me and my child in hopes that it will inspire you and your children and we can all learn and grow together. It is meant to be read as you see fit, if you're anything like me (a busy parent) than you probably don't have an entire afternoon to devote to reading this book or completing a full day of laundry! Each chapter stands alone so that you can open up to a chapter and take it from there.

Hello,

I am a beam of light to help you find your way as you navigate through this time and space.

I am the love gift from our creator sent to you as a gentle reminder, that he sees you, hears you and most of all loves you.

I am from the place, where there is no time, I am here to help you remember that once you lived there too and shall one day return.

I come wrapped in a small yet delicate form.

Because I am new to this Earth school I shall only have you to rely on. It is an enormous task but one our creator knows you can handle.

I am the precious gift from God, as you look at me please hear our fathers voice whispering softly to you that YOU are worthy, for he has entrusted one of his most sacred gifts into your unwavering hands.

As I grow and learn I shall be watching and learning from you.

One day I will be a true reflection of all that you are while you existed in this time and space.

Together we will embark upon this journey. As we travel together we shall learn many lessons together. We will learn patience, kindness, compassion, forgiveness, suffering, sacrifice and most of all we will remember love.

I am a boundless soul enclosed in a small body.

Look closer into my eyes and see the spirit of God that lives in me.

Look closer what do you see? If you look just a little closer, you will begin to see ME.

Keep looking a little while,

and you will see I have come here in the form of your child.

We are guiding evolving spirits on how to navigate their way through this Earth school.

YOU are Your Child's First Friend

We are guiding these spirits for a short time in their lives, and approaching this sacred time as someone that your child can confide in and trust builds a sense of connection with them. I had so many friends growing up whose parent's had the same "my child isn't my friend" ideology and now they are either completely estranged from their parents or have a formal relationship with them where nothing of importance is ever shared.. When we approach parenting from an authoritative perspective, our children will be fearful of sharing their hearts with us. If your goal is to get through this parenting thing with as little effort as possible and raise people who never speak to you, then by all means continue on that path.

If I have heard one phrase over and over that I'd like to erase from our culture it's this, "I am not my child's friend, I am the parent." I couldn't disagree more with this statement. It implies that parenting and friendship are mutually exclusive. When your child is first learning to walk and talk, is it not the parent they share their first laugh with, tell a joke to and confide in when something good or bad has happened to them? I don't understand this sentiment of letting your child know you aren't their friend. Not surprisingly, later on the parent is frustrated that their child doesn't share details of their life with them. As adults we don't share our thoughts and feelings with people who aren't friends so why would we expect anything different from our children?

If you envision a different path one where you and your children remain connected then take the time now to parent consciously from your whole heart.

Parents start to complain about the lack of relationship with their children when they become teenagers, yet fail to see where their personal beliefs and actions throughout the years have contributed to this disconnect.

Connection begins when they are babies, consciously learning them and who they are becoming. Let them see you not just as their parent but an evolving human being. You begin by always making eye contact with your child and acknowledging their presence by interacting with them. In being your child's first friend you show them what to expect in relationships, how it feels when someone shows you kindness, you show them what trust looks and feels like. Modeling the behavior of a friend makes it that much easier for them to learn from you through your interactions with each other.

One way that I show my son that I am his friend is by listening to him without judgment. We all have friends that we can tell anything to and it is such a comfort to know that your friend is not judging you and has nothing but love for you. How wonderful for our children to come away from any situation knowing that they are not being judged by the mistakes they make. Another way that I show my son that we are friends is by playing with him. Often as parents we are stuck in these authoritative roles and are afraid to let our children see us as someone who is a person also.

Sometimes we end up playing a game for a few hours at a time or dancing around to silly music or talking about which girl is on his marry list. The goal is to make our children feel welcome in our lives to come to us with the insignificant things early on so they will trust and confide in us the important things later on. How many children go to extreme measures to keep things from their parents because they don't feel comfortable around these people they live with who are not their friends? It could be something like a failing grade or being bullied in school and the child will feel afraid or ashamed to express themselves. It crushes my heart when I hear the news and see another child has committed suicide or run away from home. What made them feel so alone in the world that the last place they wanted to be was home with their parents. Our homes should be a place of security, love and friendship for our family. We are on this journey alongside them, so instead of feeling like we are their superior be an ally. Being their friend means listening and withholding judgment.

I grew up with friends whose parents had the mindset that if the teacher calls home the child gets an automatic beating or punishment. The parents never asked what happened, why or if it were even true. In high school we all go through a myriad of emotions as hormones are completely out of whack, we start to take on more responsibilities and get our first jobs. Having a parent/caregiver that is compassionate, kind and mindful of what is happening to teenagers can help them feel supported through these challenging years.

Finding their Passion

----

*"Do not ask your children to strive for ordinary lives. Such
striving may seem admirable but it is the way of foolishness.
Help them instead to find the wonder and the marvel of an
ordinary life. Show them the joy of tasting tomatoes, apples and
pears. Show them how to cry when pets and people die.
Show them the infinite pleasure in the touch of a hand.
And make the ordinary come alive for them.
The extraordinary will take care of itself."*
–William Martin

Our children hold our hearts for eternity and to us they will always
be our babies. Unless we have an uncanny ability to predict the
life of our children or talk to someone who does, we have no way
of knowing who our children will be as adults. When we look back
at those who have come before us we get a real sense of what
paths we can choose in raising our gifts. Our children may come
as a surprise or the careful planning of their existence, that isn't
important, what is essential is them knowing they are meant to be
here and to feel love.

There was once a boy who loved to explore his surroundings and experiment with different elements. He went on to create electricity, the phonograph and hold over 122 patents for different ideas and concepts he came up with. Because of his curiosity for life we now benefit from the numerous inventions of Thomas Edison. Betty Skelton is a name that most people haven't heard of but in the world of aeronautics she is a legend. A little girl who used to stare at airplanes flying over her house in the 1930's, became enthralled with the idea of flying. At age 8 her parents realized that flying was her passion. They made sure to expose her to multiple trips to airports in Pensacola, Florida. She talked her father into letting her fly alone in a friend's plane; at age 16 instead of obtaining her driver's license she obtained her pilots license and shortly thereafter purchased her first airplane. She became famous for performing stunts(her inverted ribbon cutting stunt is still performed at airshows today). Her Father arranged for amateur airshows to display his daughter's talent in aviation. She then went on to pursue a career in aeronautics. From airplanes she transitioned into automobiles and became involved in racing where she set a stock car speed for women. From there she launched into yet another career where she trained with NASA to be the first women to travel to space. Unfortunately although Betty Skelton completed all necessary training to go into the space the world was not yet ready. Her parents on the other hand were very ready to assist in the attainment of their daughter's dreams and passions at a time when most women were bred to be only housewives regardless of their true desires.

By their very nature, children are naturally curious about life and their experiences. Fostering their innate curious nature lends itself to co-creating creative thinkers. Children will start by exploring their immediate surroundings. When my son was a toddler, I remember he repeatedly kept trying to get in the kitchen cupboards which were secured with child safety locks. Each time he tried to get in and failed he would look so frustrated. Finally one day I gave in and opened the cabinet and he pulled out each and every frying pan and pot in there. He put a few on his head, attempted to get in one and banged on yet another. After about an hour or so, he was content that he had explored everything there was in the cabinet. He never attempted to open that cabinet again, so I learned that letting him explore his surroundings was good for him. As adults we think oh that's just a few pots and pans nothing interesting but to children it's a chance to feel new textures, and look at shiny metal objects and perhaps a new head piece. Obviously things that are dangerous for a child should always stay in a safe place away from the reach of children.

Use Everything to teach

"We teach that what we need to learn the most"
-David Bach

I'm not sure if it's because I see every moment in life as an opportunity to learn or if it's because I am always thinking and trying to see the purpose in everything. My son has been involved in sports from a very early age and has had the privilege of working with several different types of coaching throughout the years. I have attended practices and games throughout this time. Being my first child and first foray into sports I wasn't sure what to expect. Of all the coaches he's had they have all fallen somewhere in the middle being just okay, however there are two that standout for two very different reasons. The coaches that I am speaking of both taught him while he was in a younger baseball league. The first coach and his assistant would berate the team no matter if they were leading the game or if they had no points. At every practice they were told what they did wrong in the previous game. The coaches would then psyche them out and say this team we play next is really good we know we can't beat them so just try to score some runs. They would tell the children to run around the bases as though they were running from the belt and would encourage children to think about someone they are angry at and imagine they are the ball when they are swinging the bat. This perpetuates a mindset of violence and lowers their self-confidence. Anger and violence are not necessary components to produce a winning game. Practice for the most part involved the coaches working with one child and screaming at them while the other children just stood around waiting their turn. During one of the games the assistant coach screamed at the pitcher for 5 minutes straight to the point where the ref had to get involved and reprimand them. After each game whether they won or lost, the children would walk out of the dugout heads hung low, confidence left on the field and feeling in adequate. That season I spent a lot of time standing just outside the dugout trying to encourage the children and build them up. Needless to say I was happy when that season ended. I questioned whether or not to sign my son up at the same league for the next season, however in the end he wanted to play again. Some of the parents thought this method of coaching was great and welcomed and encouraged this behavior. From the sidelines parents would yell at their children or other children during the games. They said that treating them this way would make the children tough and not act like babies (the league was for 4-7 years olds). None of the children on this team seemed to be having any fun or learning about the sport.

The next coach we encountered was a total departure from everything I had seen. When I came upon the field I noticed that there were three different stations set up on the field one for catching, one for hitting and one for learning the game. The coach introduced himself and his helpers and asked each child their name (and never forgot their name or called them another child's name). He then proceeded to break the children up into small groups and work through each station. He made a game of the practice and all the children were laughing and having so much fun that they forgot they were learning. One thing that really caught my attention was the fact that three of the children were his (which I found out later on in the season) yet he treated every child as though they were all his and showed no favoritism. In previous teams when a coach had their own child on his team, that child was always the pitcher whether they wanted to be there or not. This coach had his children where he thought they could learn something new. He ended each practice and game gathering the children together in a huddle and having them repeat "no matter whether we eat or sleep or whatever we do, let it all be to the glory of GOD" I thought his style was great and was curious to see how he would respond during the season and when his team was losing. In one game my son was batting but couldn't beat the ball to first base and he looked disappointed until I saw his coach run up to him and say, nice swing buddy, you know you got that other runner home on your team- that's an RBI way to go! During a game when my son's team was winning by a rather large margin, the other team's coach (who was a 3rd base assistant) was so angry at the score that she quit in the middle of the inning, yelled a few expletives and walked off the field. Not missing a beat the coach had his brother in law(who helped out during practices) step in for my son's team and told the other children he would be their 3rd base coach for the remainder of the game. Throughout that season I continued to watch the coach be an inspiration to the children, parents and other coaches. During tournament time, my son's team lost their first game, after which some of the children were bummed realizing the steep mountain they had to climb. Coach J took them aside and said listen I have no doubt that if we would've had a few more minutes we could've changed some things. "Do not be deterred, tomorrow you guys will have to win all 4 games in order to win the championship. I know it can be done and you guys are the ones to do it. Never forget that with GOD, all things are possible." I thought to myself that is so sweet of the coach to give these children some hope to hold on to but there's no way they can do that, maybe they will win one or two games but surely not all 4 games. The end of the next day arrived and they just kept winning every game and when they won the championship game you would've never known. Their coach had taught them not to brag and boast so when they won they quietly went to the other team and shook hands and told them how well they had played. Now my son is on yet another team and using what he learned from his former coach he inspires his teammates, whenever they come into the dugout he will say great RBI or slap them high five, he tells the other teams how well they did also. Through being around that coach, he taught the children patience, teamwork, encouragement and learning through failure. Those children started out playing unsure of themselves and their abilities and finished the season with new confidence in themselves and their capabilities. When showing the children the way it is imperative not to become deadset on outcomes but to always keep the children in our hearts and minds first. Winning or losing a game is not important in the scheme of life but building up a child's self-esteem and learning to face failures with grace and humility is the point.

Activities

"The creation of something new is not accomplished by the intellect but by the play instinct acting from inner necessity. The creative mind plays with objects it loves."
-C.G. Jung

Childhood should be a magical time, a place where love is at the center, where dreams are first created. A place of peace that children will carry with them into the world to leave it a better place than the one they were born into. Using their imagination as often as possible lets them be limitless when it comes to their potential.

When I was pregnant and learned that I was having a boy, I felt as though I was giving birth to some other species. I was never a super girly girl nor was I a tomboy yet still I couldn't envision a life with "boy-things." I had heard stories about those rambunctious, high energy, getting into everything kinds of children and was frightened at the prospect of having one of those, so of course if you focus so much on what you don't want- guess what? That is exactly what I received.

When my little guy began to think his own thoughts and discover life outside of just his family he became curious about the world in which we live. Around 2 or 3 years old children begin asserting themselves and making statements as to their wants needs, likes dislikes and more often than not, their introduction to the word no!

I approached this phase of moving from infant to toddler as I did with many others, I put myself in my child's shoes. Initially I was thrown off by this new behavior of perceived defiance and assertiveness, however then I thought about myself in terms of what children experience at this stage. It's like moving to a foreign country where you don't speak the language and everyone is a stranger, yet everyone is looking at you and telling you what to do. If I were in a foreign country, I would first have to learn the language once I understand that I can move into the phase of learning the culture and idiosyncrasies of that country. I would be curious and hope there would be someone (a native) to learn from. After 2 or 3 years I would feel comfortable venturing out into some new territory and exploring my surrounding's. If I found a word in this new language that I liked I would say often. This is the life of a toddler, everything is colorful, new (to them), strange, and a little scary as they have now mastered walking and are no longer as physically dependent on the parents for mobility. This is a time to let them be wanderers of all things and to observe what they are drawn to and listen to what they are saying.

Experiencing life through a child's eyes can help us learn new things about different subjects that we never gave a second thought about and can open us up to wonderful experiences. When it comes to a child's interests, letting them lead the way can foster confidence in themselves and create an enthusiasm for learning.

When my son was almost 2 he developed a liking (or obsession) for all things trains. I saw this as a learning opportunity for both of us. We dove in and learned every fact that I could find on trains, who invented them, which type, what they run on, where they go etc. We immersed ourselves in train books, cartoons and museums. Following that phase he moved into dinosaurs and we learned of the classification of the different species, when they lived what they ate, how they died.

It is our responsibility to guide them and expose them to as many different areas of life so that they can make up their own minds when the time comes. Our children are the leaders of tomorrow therefor it is imperative to assist them with unlocking their passion and calling.

In our family we watch many documentaries and read books on everything from Monster Trucks, How the Universe Works, Strip the City, Brain Games and Nikola Tesla. We have in depth conversations about each thing that we watch and discuss how we can relate to those people and what our take away is from that documentary.

We all want our children to have fun and experience new and exciting things. I know it can be quite pricey when gathering up a family of four or more to go to an amusement park or family outing of any kind. When your finances are tied up but you have a desire for your child to experience things, there are many options that are affordable or free. My biggest resource has been our public library. From the time my son was only 18 months old we have been active members at our local library. Local libraries offer story times for most ages 10 and under. In addition to story time, some libraries also give families special discounts at museums or theatres. The library also has different activities that may correspond to different holidays and themes that offer unique opportunities to learn new things. In addition to our local library some of the museum's in our closest city offer free days each month. It may be worthwhile to invest in a membership to a zoo, aquarium or museum that you and your children love and enjoy going to. Personally memberships have come in handy, especially because some of them offer tickets for two adults and an unlimited children under 18 that means you and another Parent friend and their children, no matter how many. That means if you have extended family staying over a holiday and want to get out of the house for a while and is looking for something fun to do, going to that place is an option. Some of the museums and membership programs transfer to other states as well so if you happen to be visiting family or friends, your little ones still have something fun to do. If you're more of an outdoor parent, then a park is your best bet. Not only do national parks offer spectacular views and free play they are a chance for you and your children to be present with each other and connect to nature through your surroundings. Guided tours at National parks and day trips to farms are ways for children to learn about their local agriculture and geography.

Today we have so many technology devices we barely notice our surrounding's anymore. In previous generations, we didn't make any effort to notice wildlife and explore outside, it was our everyday existence. Sure we have many conveniences but at the core it seems something innocent has been lost. Gone are the days when children were just outside until dark with no schedule, a curfew and no supervision. Now parents set up playdates where the activity is structured for a set amount of time but between school and the myriad of lessons, playdates are far and few between. It is vital that our children know the outside world like they know technology. Take them outside to lie in the grass and gaze up at the clouds or take them to an observatory to view the night sky to see the planets firsthand through a telescope. Let them feel the awe at having an encounter with a wild animal or taste the first drops of snow on a cold winter's night. Camping out is a wonderful time to spend time exploring, connecting with each other and being in nature.

Technology isn't going away at least for the foreseeable future so instead of banning it completely (which only makes people want something more), incorporate ways to virtually connect with family. You can Facetime your children throughout the day if possible. With younger children instead of handing them our tablets to busy themselves with, find games or apps that are set up for more than one player and spend the time with them instead of letting them play alone.

As a by-product of exploring many different activities and interests our children will develop a love of learning. If we expose our children to many things their true nature will guide them to what it is that sets their hearts on fire.

Rather than shunning technology or saying it is bad, we could consciously embrace it and use it to connect with our children more. Play games with your children on their gaming consoles, teach them how to use different aspects of your phones and tablets and use that as a time to connect with them.

Educate

"Just as a gardener helps the tree, you cannot pull on the tree
to make it grow fast; you cannot do anything in that way, nothing
can be done positively. You plant the seed, you water, you give
the manure, an d you wait! The tree happens on its own. When
the tree is happening you protect it so somebody does not hurt
it or harm it. That is the function of a teacher: the teacher has to
be a gardener. Now that you have to create the child; the child is
coming on its own, existence is the creator."
-Osho

Academics are important but allowing them the space to uncover
their passion and calling through unrestricted play, creativity
and arts are also important in developing our children as a whole
person. It is through the act of play and having fun that your
mind is in a state to receive and process new information. In some
preschools the concept of learning through play is emphasized
and the children enjoy playing for the day not realizing all that
they are learning.

Children are now being pushed at such young ages to
memorize concepts, grasp new techniques and perform well on

standardized test and in addition the common core standards that public schools are mandated to adhere to. Teachers are pushed to move children through topics at lightning speed or face being reprimanded if their student's test scores are low. Some teachers have even gone as far as altering a student's test to avoid these low score. I can't help but have sympathy for the pressure the teachers are under these days-not to mention the children. The idea that one test (or several over a short period of time) can fully grasp the all encompassing ever-changing nurturing spirit of our children is ridiculous, but that's a whole other issue best left for another time. There are studies everywhere that state how children are performing poorly because of stress and standardized tests. If a subject is interpreted as boring, learning about it can be agonizing for a child. If we can ignite their imagination and use that as a tool in the classroom, learning becomes a side effect of their active imagination. While it is true that children spend the majority of their time learning from a teacher (if you decide to go that route), it is still up to us as parents to pass along information that we feel is important. If our teachers have missed something, we need to fill in the gap and create and an ongoing dialogue about learning and school.

Society as a whole seems focused on outcomes/results rather than experience. It is worth noting that each child receives information in a different way. Public schools seem to streamline learning to make it advantageous to a certain type of learner. There are multiple learning styles, they are commonly labeled under the acronym V.A.R.K. V.A.R.K. stands for Verbal, Aural, Reading/writing and Kinesthetic. Verbal learners are children who learn through speaking, A is for Aural learners who learn through hearing material, R stands for reading/writing, these learners grasp concepts through reading then writing what they have learned and finally K stands for Kinesthetic learners who learn through doing i.e., field trips and making things. My son is a verbal learner which means essentially his brain receives information best when he is able to talk about information to another person or to talk out loud to himself. I on the other hand learn through reading and taking copious notes. When I assist my son with his homework I take into account his learning style and structure it to reinforce enrichment activities through games or songs I create. Many parents complain when their children are struggling in school and though the teacher is the designated educator, they are not the primary source for where your children can learn.

Wwhen I was in elementary school I loved math, until 3rd grade. In 3rd grade I was introduced to the concept multiplication and division. My teacher worked with me diligently however the concepts seemed just beyond my grasp. Thankfully that year my family moved to another town and I started a new school. I will never forget my 3rd grade teacher Ms. Magglio. She was a spicy Italian divorcee who brought her spunky personality to everything she taught us. When we reached the dreaded multiplication issue, she took a new approach. Instead of using hard cold facts and how many two's make 6, she played an old record player of songs for multiplication. Music is one of my greatest passions, so I memorized the songs and never forgot it. To this day if I have to perform a multiplication task I hear parts of the song in my head to reach an answer. I have now taken that same approach in regards to my son's learning. When he is learning new words, we will come up with a rhyme, poem or short song to make learning it simple. When the concept of multiplication is introduced I will no doubt pass on that useful tool I learned many years ago. I understand that music may not work for everyone. However I know that our ability to learn is limitless once we introduce our imagination into playing with the material.

When I go to the library some afternoons, it is always filled with parents and their children seated at desks doing homework. No matter which day I attend, I walk past and I always see and hear the same thing. A child having a hard time grasping a subject and looking frustrated, the parent repeating the same material and adding a threat, such as, if you don't spell this right you are not playing outside when we get home. Sadly it doesn't look like much fun for the parent or the child. If we take on a frustrated approach to helping them succeed they may adopt our same attitude and belief. We want to encourage and inspire them with learning not berate them for something they are struggling with. A more effective approach to feeling frustrated with our children's progress is to change our perspective. For example if your children are struggling with reading and learning their vocabulary words, create a song or melody that inserts the spelling of the word.

Learning of course takes place in the classroom but that is just a small aspect of a child's life. Learning really happens anywhere that we go or whomever we're around. While homeschooling my son we used life as our classroom. Going to the park and looking at the insects and landscape or discussing a budget while grocery shopping or going to a certain destination and having him direct us back home to learn more about directions and making landmarks.

Some parents are attending higher education later on in life after they've started their families. If you are in that group share with your family what you are learning in a way that they can receive it and if they are old enough engage in a conversation with them about a topic you find fascinating. It will open them up to the idea of higher learning and also make them feel smart among their friends when they discuss something with confidence that they learned from one of your classes.

Children today are so blessed to have the advantage of technology as they mature and find their own calling. Thankfully there are many children who aren't waiting until they are adults to fulfill their dreams. I watched a brilliant Tedx talk by a 10 year old (at the time) girl in India named Ishita Katyal. She told the story of how she attended a Ted talk with her mother when she was a few years younger and had been inspired by the things she could understand. She decided to start a Ted talk for children and also become an author. Her perspective was that adults always ask children what do they want to do when they grow up and basically leave them pining away for the future instead of doing what they want now. Just because children are young doesn't mean they don't know what they want or how to achieve it.

If your child is drawn to a certain path, encourage them and assist them in bringing forth their vision. My son likes to write his own stories about robots, woodcutters and the like. Sometimes he will write them down or I will bind them into a little book so that he has a physical copy of it and knows that he is capable of doing something at this age.

One day I was watching a show called Shark Tank, which is a show where entrepreneur's pitch business ideas and the "sharks"(billion and millionaire's) decide if they will invest in a business. This particular day there was a young boy on the show who had a passion for making bow ties. His charming personality and business acumen won over all the sharks and though they didn't give him an investment; however one of the sharks decided to mentor him. His business eventually went on to earn $250,000.

When seeking education for future leaders they will need to encompass intelligence yes but also compassion, awareness, creativity and kindness.

Walking your Talk

Children are born knowing the bare essentials when they are infants. Everything they think and how they act they are initially imitating you. Whether it's trying on makeup like Mommy or watching sports like Daddy. For most of their formative years children learn how to be from their parents/caregivers. It's important to not only mean what you tell your children but to follow that same advice for yourself. I have always taught my son to be respectful of himself and with other children. I've explained different scenarios to him and the consequences of certain actions. Until your child has an opportunity to display what they have learned you're not sure if they really understand. One day I dropped my son off at a children's fun zone inside of the gym where I worked out. I went upstairs and worked out for the next hour. When I picked my son up he had a peculiar look on his face and he admitted in the car that some kids had been mean to him and said some hurtful things. Seeing my son upset automatically put me into Mama bear mode and I stooped to a low level and said some not so nice things in the moment to which T replied, well I think I will just pray for them because something must be wrong with them and I know it has nothing to do with me (he was only 3 at the time), my mouth just dropped open and I was left speechless. Later that evening I shared our conversation on a social media website and I said that I was so surprised at his response and one of my friends said, "Well done Mom, he's just saying all the good things you're putting into him." Then I thought back on the different books I've read and other times when I've used challenges as opportunities and was proud of myself knowing that. I have taught my child to forgive quickly and how to love boldly.

Never make a promise that you can't keep. This is a rule that I've learned growing through my experiences with broken promises. One day our sweet little children will be adults operating in society and creating their own lives so making sure that we instill in them core qualities is paramount. I always tell my son if I tell you I'm going to do something then I'm going to do it period. I tell him integrity is important in building a trusted bond with someone. There have been promises that I thought why did I make that promise or it's inconvenient right now or maybe I'll just break it this once but I always think about how way leads to way. I know that if I break it even one time that I am slowly teaching my son something different than my intention. Whenever he learns something new he'll say, "Is that true Mom and based on my response he will accept this new idea whole heartedly or reject it and never question it. Because I have his full trust I feel a sense of obligation to find what the truth is so that I know I am giving him the best of me.

Kids have a natural inclination to sift through our b.s., point it out and then call you on your crap. If you want your children to possess certain quality's it is imperative for them to witness you displaying those characteristics. Telling a child not to gossip or bully sounds good but if they witness you and your friends talking about your other friends or colleagues they witness you being inauthentic. In no way am I implying that we are to be perfect. Obviously we all make mistakes and that is a part of the journey we are all on. In times when we find ourselves displaying attributes that go against our teachings we should let our children know that we made a mistake. This subject includes all areas of life. Young girls model their behavior and how they respond to their bodies from the women in their lives. If Mom and her friends constantly obsess over dieting trends and their weight than you can bet your daughter will replicate this behavior with her friends. Boys will do the same thing with their fathers or the men in their life.

Discipline

"An eye for an eye makes the whole world blind"
-Wayne Dyer

For many of us we have been raised to believe that the word children and discipline are synonymous. Coming from a Christian upbringing I was taught by family members "spare the rod, spoil the child" which to me just meant didn't make sense.

At least once a week I'll see a meme or someone rant on a social media website stating that the problem with children is that they aren't getting beat enough and how when they were children themselves they were beat and now they are these great people. If we thought about that statement in terms of two adults, one would never say to his friends "man, the problem with your wife is that you aren't' beating her enough," or "spare the rod, spoil the wife." Any person who voiced such an opinion would be labeled as obnoxious, ignorant and controlling, however when parents say that about our children we are expected to say that's right, that's why I beat my children every time they step out of line.

In my opinion, physical discipline is ineffective in guiding a conscious developing person. As adults we tend to view other adults as our equals. We are often in situations where conflict arises and do we say to ourselves let me put my boss, spouse, friend or whomever in timeout or they need my discipline. We don't say that because the idea of putting another adult in timeout sounds absolutely ridiculous. Instead of putting a coworker or friend in timeout you would find an effective solution to resolve the conflict. That is the same way our children should be treated. You aren't raising a child, the formative years only last 18 years they are an adult for the rest of their life. You are guiding an evolving spirit on how to navigate their way through this Earth school.

It is surprising to me that people think nothing of stating that they beat their kids but are appalled at hearing of a spouse who abuses the other one. Why is it okay to beat our children into submission to do what we say but not our beloved husband or wife?

Some children are taught as a child that when you do something wrong it is okay and even beneficial for you to feel pain from authority all in the name of love. When that child becomes a teenager and engages with people they feel desensitized to pain as it has become commonplace. Now when we see someone behaving "badly" it is justifiable for them to be hit. Violence of any kind wrongs and wounds both individuals since we are all connected.

The biggest defense of physical abuse or discipline is that hey it achieves results i.e. the child responded and stopped said behavior. I want to ask, what have you really accomplished by abusing your position of power over a small defenseless child by hitting them into submission? The only thing you have accomplished is distorting their view of pain and twisted it into a warped meaning of love.

It is baffling to me that many believe that without discipline the children of the world would run amuck and not be raised to respect authority.

Time-outs were pretty interesting for my parenting journey. I thought to myself he will stand in time out and think about why he's in there and get it. Really, it just became a time for me to cool down and refocus my energy on the true issue at hand and not being reactive. My son would do something perceived to be wrong and then say he was going to go put himself in time out. One day he admitted that he wasn't thinking about his undesired act or behavior but rather coming up with new ideas in his head to pass the time more quickly. He spent no time thinking on that incident, so instead of pushing our children away when we deem an undesired action why not pull them in close and talk with them to create an understanding of why we are upset or why their sibling is crying. I saw a post on a social media site where the parent listens to music with various uses of profanity in it and her 2 year old began singing the same lyrics Mom was singing and she smacked her child in the mouth. That is very confusing to a child, especially when they see their parent doing/saying something and make an attempt to emulate them but get disciplined because of it. Children learn the most from our own behaviors not our opinions.

There is an alternative to physical discipline and that is that they learn to govern themselves. This approach may not be as favorable because it takes time, patience, imperfection and an open heart. Here are two incidents that completely changed the way I parented my own child. One Father's day I was in a coffee shop overlooking a pristine lake, the coffee house was quaint with a bohemian laid back atmosphere. A cozy fire place sat in the middle unlit as it was unnecessary in June, intimate seating options and the latest of some unknown jazz artist playing in the background. The door opens and in walks two little girls with the prettiest dresses with little ringlets of curls to match their bouncing steps through the shop. They came zipping through in a fury running up to the stand to see what goodies had been made that morning, they then took off toward a huge window that overlooked the lake squealing with delight as they took in the lake's majestic nature. About 30 seconds behind them came the obviously doting grandparents and then Mom and the 6 month old baby. The adult trio with baby in tow went to the barista and ordered their food and brought it to their table and sat down to eat and at the same time the girls are continuing to scream, jump and laugh madly at each new discovery they saw in the lake below. I thought to myself at any moment grandma or grandpa are going to get them to sit down and stop being so noisy and tell them to come eat. Instead the girls ran around laughed picked up a lady bug, took it outside and went back to looking out the window and yelling then one said to the others, let's get something to eat. They sat down quietly to eat their food. I was amazed that the children all got up from the window and sat down to eat. They proceeded to sit quietly and talk in hushed tones, giggling here and there as they ate. As they were about to leave, one of the girls said she wanted something else to eat and her Mom said you have to choose something that your sister wants also. The two of them talked it over (between the ages of 3-5) said well I think we should get this because you like it and the other said the same thing. They made the decision between them and told their Mom their choice. Never once did the Mom intervene to yell at the girls, to make them eat their food or tell them what they were going to eat or tell them to not run or be quiet. When we let our children govern themselves, they will do what feels right to them.

The strangest thing of all is that I had the exact opposite experience in a different coffee house the night before. It was a Friday night and this particular chain coffee house sold wine and it became a lounge scene in the evenings. Across from me were two couples, one with 2 children and one without. The parents sat with their friends at one end of the table and put their children at the opposite end. The children appeared to be between 7-12 years of age, both were quietly playing on smart phones or tablets. I thought to myself look at those cute children playing so quietly, wow. About 10 minutes later the younger one goes to the restroom and the father approaches the older child and yells at her for not throwing out her trash however once she does that he then yells at her for letting the 7 year old go to the restroom alone. He then yanks her up and demands that she get the brother from the restroom. I'll never forget the look on the children's faces when they returned from the restroom; it was a look of pure terror. Once seated the children whisper back and forth between them to which the father tells them to shut up. They sank further into their seats and resumed play on their devices. Throughout their time at the coffee shop, the Father continued to give them directions and tell them what they were doing wrong. From what I could tell the Father was unable to enjoy time with his friends and the children were unable to enjoy there's as well.

After witnessing both experiences almost back to back I began to seriously reconsider the method of discipline I had learned from family members as a child. It was evident that the children I had seen Friday night obeyed their Father out of fear and terror. It was also evident that the children the next day had the freedom to live life on their terms and overall appeared to enjoy themselves that day. I thought about the outcomes of both sets of children and decided it was in the best interest of my child/children to explore their world and to be themselves.

In the community I was raised in, it is heavily frowned upon if you don't whip your children or punch them or assert authority over them at all times especially in public. The messages I hear so often are; keep your child in check, let them know who's boss, fearing your parent is healthy, I always felt so good after a nice beating! Seriously!! It is outrageous to me that common sense goes out the window in regards to our children. Society would be up in arms if a woman said I always feel great and have a nice cry after my husband has punched/beat me. The reason I keep referring to domestic abuse in regards to physical discipline of our children because there is no distinction. Hitting anything is always wrong, period. There have been many times in public my son has had meltdowns or he's been over stimulated in the environment and without fail, there are always the looks that silently say I know she's going to wear him out or she better beat him. When I do nothing or respond with compassion and apologize to my son saying something like, "I know bud, I'm sorry I kept you out too long today and you didn't have your nap but we'll get home soon." It is no longer a concern of mine what the stranger next to me thinks about my child's behavior or my response to it, what does matter to me is how my child feels. Does he feel safe with me, does he know beyond the shadow of a doubt that he is loved?

Instead of the time outs or physical discipline I simply talk with my child to teach him about life. It requires more time on our parts, to get down to their level and really talk them through what is going on and to assist them through their thoughts and feelings. When my son was younger I caught him hitting one of our family pets and instead of yelling go to timeout or hitting him for hitting the cat. I'll sit him down and ask how did that make you feel when you hit the cat? Based on his response that it felt good to hit the cat, and then I asked how do you think the cat feels now? His reply was I never thought about it, I said well let's sit and think about how it feels to just sit somewhere and out of the blue you are hit by someone, he said that would be awful. Then he confessed, well I only did it because I was upset I couldn't play on your computer. Let's say he says it felt good to hit the cat, then I would bring to his attention look you feel good but now they don't trust you and won't come near you. Is that what you were trying to accomplish, to make the cat afraid of you? You know the cats trust you to look out for them and to be their guardian but now they aren't so sure since you hit them.

I felt like an amateur in Motherhood and felt the pressure of those scornful eyes, judging what I would do. As a parent you have more than likely experienced some of those scornful looks also. It is understandable there are times when it can be mortifying when our children are calling what is perceived as negative attention to us, in those moments it is tempting to conform to others opinions.

I did resort to what I perceived as pressure and would respond to my son in a very unloving manner. I would give him a little pinch and whisper, "get it together you're embarrassing me", which would only make him more upset but I would see I had the approval of others in the room. Thankfully, I gave up caring what others think and now focus on just being present for my son and making sure that he knows that I am here for his highest self not my ego's desire for approval from strangers.

Balance

"Lend yourself to others, but give yourself to yourself."
-Michele de Montaigne

I can tell you from experience that balance is something I struggle with daily. Being a mother is such a fulfilling role and you get to visually watch the manifestation of all your hard work exhibited in the world, beings you helped co-create. I constantly have to remind myself of the instruction they give you just before take-off on an airplane. Put your own mask on first or else you can't help your child if you yourself can't breathe. Being a mother though is not our only role in life so just as you devote time to being Jenny's Mom or the Mom of twins it is just as important to devote time to YOU. We are teaching our children about life, love, existence, happiness and socialization. What better way to teach than by being. As I said being a Mom can be isolating at times especially if you're among the first of your friends or community to begin a family. The internet is really great for finding a community of people who share your same interests. Devoting time to you and your interests can be as big as a girls only get away to a beautiful destination or something as simple as going to a coffee shop alone and reading a book or taking a nice walk in nature. Connecting with our spouses, children and family is necessary and staying connected to you is vital. Some times it's easy to get into the auto pilot zone where one day melds into the next and there is relatively little thinking done concerning the activities you are doing but is important to stay mindful.

As my son gets older, we delve constantly into new territory and each new chapter brings with it opportunities disguised as challenges. When you're child's strong willed personality shows itself you are faced with opposition. As a baby my son never cried, a never for not a bottle or to be changed. I didn't hear him cry until he was around 2 and he decided he in the middle of the shopping mall to get in someone else's cart but to first throw the other persons bags on the floor. I must say I was quite literally shocked. At the time I was so angry, that when we came home I had to seek a few minutes of solace so that I didn't do or say something I would later regret Thankfully I can recall those moments now with a gleam in my eye and a smile in my heart. Children will test your patience until you feel you've had enough and then they push you even farther. The worst thing we can do is to give in to our feelings of anger and lash out at these precious souls. But admit it, sometimes it happens!! If you do find yourself in a fit of rage or your stomach knotted with anger and before you know it, you've said something in anger to your child- don't beat yourself up about it. We are all human and still learning this delicate dance of parenting. It has happened to me more than once. Once I've calmed down I take my son aside and explain to him that his behavior could've been different and that I chose the wrong response by responding that way and I apologize for my actions and then I ask for his forgiveness. It is important for me to let my son know that I am not a machine and won't always get it right myself but that I am always a willing participant to achieving peace. Letting our children see that we are not always right or perfect allows them to know that they are okay when they do something wrong. We are not trying to craft the perfect human being but rather a person who is attuned to their thoughts and feelings and is secure in themselves. The other day I heard yelling and screaming outside the front of my house and when I looked across the street I could see my neighbor berating his daughter. It was the worst feeling; his daughter just took in every word and probably internalized it. He stood there for two or more hours just ripping her to pieces, mocking her movements, yelling in her face and all over basketball as if the entire reason for her existence is to put a ball in a net. If our children do or don't do something it's very tempting to give in to our anger lash out, hit them or whatever avenue seems most convenient in the moment. Each time we do that, we are forever changing our children's lives and even scaring them. Our children have been loaned to us for a while; we don't own or control them. If ever you try to control children they will only follow out of fear. Loving them through the difficult stages requires some growth on everyone's part. I hate when I get on a social media website and I see people posting things like "here are my troublemakers" or here are my "bad kids" or they are bratty or just unkind things. People assume that children are born knowing everything about how this world works. Which isn't the case? Children are figuring out so much and their brains and little bodies are just trying to take everything in. A good way to teach your children is to talk to them constantly about everything. If you can find a book about it, read it to them (it really does make a difference). When my son was one I brought him several Halloween books and explained to him what Halloween was and what we do as a tradition. So when Halloween came he was 15 months old, I took him trick-or-treating and he couldn't speak in sentences yet so I was prepared to give the neighbors his bucket and say trick or treat, I was totally surprised when we got to the first house and he handed them his bucket and said a word that he could manage at his age "boo." I was so delighted because it let me know that he had been listening and while he couldn't say everything I knew he understood what this was. Initially I thought it was just a fluke however when we arrived at the next house he said the same thing. I did the same thing when it came to other holidays and things that I hold important in my family. I have found that once a child understands why or what they typically comply. This concept was especially important when it came time to potty train him. Thankfully, around the time I potty trained my son there was a song called the Potty dance which helped us tremendously. There were also a multitude of books and interactive guides that assisted me with allowing him to understand the concepts of where and how we deposit our bodily waste.

Take it all in

I understand that as new parents or parents attempting to implement a different way of parenting into your lifestyle that some things may not resonate with you and and that's okay. There is no one size fits all perfect parenting technique that works for each child and parent combination. It is our task to figure out what works best for our children and keeps us at least a little sane!

Teaching our children how to handle their emotions sets them up to be emotionally stable and capable of navigating themselves through the different emotions that will arise and experience in life. One technique that I use with my son is that when he is angry I tell him to take that anger he is experiencing, to blow it out in an imaginary balloon and send it up into the sky so that the anger doesn't steal his eternal joy. It's important for our children to know that having an outlet for their emotions helps them move through them. We all learn by either going through things ourselves or from listening to others who have paved the way graciously for us. There are only two ways of learning either through joy or pain. How we respond to life's challenges dictates how we learn. The great thing is that if we are learning through pain, the moment we become conscious of this fact we can shift our way into joy. Emotions are a normal part of our being and energy; it's how we deal with these emotions that make the difference. Creating a space for an emotional outlet allows children to experience that feeling and then letting it go so that it doesn't carry over into other aspects of their live. If the imaginary balloon tactic isn't working for your beloved child then try another. Younger children and older ones can benefit from this simple practice.

These processes work best however when explained to them prior to them feeling these emotions. Writing down their thoughts and feelings about what is currently happening is a great way for them to express what is occurring and the final step being to rip up the paper and let it go. For younger ones, just getting out the old crayons, markers and just drawing a picture of what they are feeling is a variation if reading and writing hasn't begun yet. This is also a great practice for parents as well. Prior to becoming a parent I hadn't picked up a crayon since elementary school, however one day my son asked me to color with him and although I was internally stressed out that day, I sat and colored with him. I ended up releasing the feelings of stress and slipped into a more relaxed state of being. Now it is an activity I really enjoy and it also helps quiet my mind and I am spending quality time with my little guy.

Parents as Partners

"Listen to what little children have to say.
We may find they have more to teach us than us them"
The Paradigm Shift

This view of a parent is one that will assist in fostering a spiritually awakened child. I hate to break it to you parents, that while we may know a lot of things and may hold various degrees from here or there, we do not know it all. Treating our children as though we are the "be all end all" of everything creates in them a sense that what they may think, feel or have to say isn't important. Often times we can learn our most valuable lessons from our little ones, who are in unique positions as they have just come here from "somewhere." In some ways they are more connected to truth than we are as they are trailing the breath of the master's. When many of our beloved children are able to speak sentences they will say things that are so profound or remember when they lived before this time.

My cousin who had the most happy, beautiful bright spirit about him used to always say (at only 3 years old) before I used to be an alcoholic and I used to party a lot(things he had never heard of in this time). He spoke of his previous life every day until he was around 5 or 6 and then I recall asking him about his previous life and he had no recollection anymore. In the Hindu religion it is believed that the soul reincarnates into another body when babies are born. Each child gets their head shaved at 1 or 3 years old to cleanse them of this past life so that they can experience life anew.

Quite honestly I believed in these things as a child, however as I grew older and the doldrums of the real world set in, I stopped believing. Since GOD has a great sense of humor, GOD of course sent me a child who couldn't be more of my opposite if he tried. When my son was born I was quite confused because he never seemed to be a baby by the standards I had witnessed growing up. He seemed as though he were looking right at me or through me sometimes and often I would catch him appearing as though he were thinking. I read several new parent books on babies and none of them mentioned what he was doing.

At 4 months old I took my son to a friend's birthday party and I was concerned about taking him to the basement where the actual party was taking place so I kept him upstairs sequestered in a separate part of the house. I kept saying the noise will be too much for him, there are too many people here, we should just go back home. About an hour into the party, I was hungry and resigned myself to going downstairs quickly and then rushing him back up the steps, however going back upstairs never happened. When we made it downstairs my son let out the biggest burst of laughter I had ever heard and I thought he was scared so I went to head back upstairs however he started to cry so I turned back toward the basement and he smiled again. I took a seat on the far part of the room so as not to expose him to the music and people and much to my surprise he started trying to move to the music and even threw his hands up and smiled at everyone he saw. One lady sat next to me and quickly smiled at him, to say that he was captivated by her is a gross understatement, he was obsessed with her and spent the rest of the evening on her lap. When I tried to offer him his bottle he looked at me like I'm with the lady here, I don't want that baby thing" and proceeded to slap it from my hands. About an hour into the party, everyone in the room became aware of him. People kept asking me, how old is he? He seems like he's really enjoying this party and he's so alert. I have so many more of these stories I could write a book about it. It was these early experiences that he and I shared that have allowed me to see him as my equal. He is nothing less than the love and light God created him to be. He has been entrusted to my care and it is my duty to keep him aware of who he is. While I pride myself on knowing a few things, I relish in the fact that I can learn from him. I told him I was writing this book, so last night at bed time he says, "I would like to offer some advice on parenting with love. " He went on to say, "Parents, whipping your child is not good for them, it makes them feel like the world is a dark and gloomy place." I asked, "So what is it you think parents should do instead, or let's say the parent is really frustrated and have asked their child several times to do something and they aren't listening?" His reply came quickly, "Oh that's easy, just say Dear Child, I really need you to do this. If the parents really explain things to their child, it makes it easier. Actually the parent could make up a song, poem or game so that they will do what their parents want. The way I see it, parenting should be fun." Out of the mouths of babes!

As a child I was often around my grandparents and great grandparents and they were of the old mindset that children should be seen and not heard, speak when spoken to and children have nothing important to say. If a grownup needed something we were basically just an errand child and our only hope was once we became a little older, the younger children in the family would take over the role of errand child. In being partners with your child, you help the child to bond with you and to view you as a real person not an authority figure. This next technique actually came into existence from my own Mom with my son. One night he was with her and was acting rambunctious as a little ones can be some times. He said oh I bet my Mommy never acted like this, Mommy was perfect right? My Mom proceeded to share with him stories about different things from my childhood. To emphasize a lesson on listening to your parents when it's for your own good, my Mom shared a story about when I was 5 years old and was having my very first sleepover. I was so excited I could barely contain myself, I kept running through the house looking at decorations and I couldn't keep my eyes or hands off my cake. My great grandma had made it and it was perfect. My Mom told me several times, Venus leave the cake alone. I just couldn't keep my eyes off of it. My Mom moved the cake to a shelf high in our dining room. While she wasn't looking, I grabbed a chair reached up and grabbed the cake, I just wanted to look at it. As expected my little hands couldn't support the size of the cake and it went right out of my hands onto the floor. I was devastated and my Mom (hearing a splat sound) came rushing in and said, Venus didn't I tell you not to touch the cake anymore. I could go buy you a cake from the grocery store but you didn't listen so I can't reward negative behavior. My friends arrived a few hours later, and when it was time for cake and ice cream, we only had ice cream. My Mom said, "Venus why don't you tell your friends why there isn't any cake." Upon hearing that story, my Mom said my son seemed so relieved and even the next day when she asked him to do something he said, oh I better do it or I could end up like Mommy did when she was little.

Looking back my own Mom never used the words conscious parenting or awakened but her approach in our community received plenty of negative feedback. When issues arose in our house the first thing my Mom did was talk to us about it and explain in detail why certain things were important. For instance when I was in kindergarten my cousin and I told a lie. We decided to lie on our school principal and tell our parents that the principal beat us (this was back when schools were just abolishing corporal punishment). Thinking(or not thinking) it was just a small lie and that it would blow over quickly my cousin and I were surprised when my Mom and her best friend had taken the day off from work and showed up at our school. I saw my Mom, her best friend, the principal and two other adults outside of our classroom talking in a heated discussion. My Mom looked through the glass classroom door, saw my face and knew we had lied. She had me removed from the classroom and said we will talk about this later, I have to get in to work since there is no real issue here. Later at home my Mom asked, Venus why did you lie? I of course had no idea why I lied. I shrugged my shoulders and my Mom said the wisest thing to me. She said it's really a shame that you lied because up until this point everything you told me I believed but now that you have told this one lie that involved a lot of people, I have to question everything you tell me from now on. She said, "no matter what happens or what you say I have to now ask myself is Venus telling the truth because the foundation of trust that we were building with each other now has a crack in it." I was devastated and her words had a profound impact on the rest of my life. Now I am known in my family as the one who tells the truth, though I could use a little finesse with my honesty. My Mom never once lost her cool, screamed or hit me for that instead she used it as a unique opportunity to teach me the importance of being honest. She explained how once you tell one lie than you have to tell more lies to cover up the first one and the more lies you tell the more bizarre the story sounds until you can't think of anything but trying to keep all your lies straight. I went to bed that night and made a vow to myself that I would always be honest with my Mom so that she would know that she could trust me. I understand the importance of being a person of integrity and that to build trust with your parents and children it takes small acts of vulnerability.

Guiding our children and being their partners on this path is about respecting them as beings who have something to offer this world. Often time's children are viewed as not having any real value because they don't yet possess the knowledge of an encyclopedia. A child's point of view holds just as much relevance (maybe even more) than an adults. Growing up my great grandparents were of the mindset children should only speak when spoken to and taught that all people who were older than us deserve respect. My Mom on the contrary taught us that we deserved respect too, she said no matter what anyone else says I am telling you that respect is a two way street. I always remembered that and although at times it made my grandparents cringe it helped me develop self worth.

As a teenager I would drive to my grandfather's house to cook him breakfast because it was hard for him to move around and just about every morning he would say some of the cruelest things to me, he would say them in a joking manner but after hearing it so many times, it began to take its toll on me until finally one day I had enough. I said "Pop-pop, listen I am here to make you breakfast and the whole time I do it you are berating me, if you call me one more name I am dropping this spatula and leaving immediately! To my surprise, he burst into tears saying he didn't know he was hurting my feelings, he apologzied and never called me another name.

The one statement I see over and over on social media is that children these days don't respect authority. I always wonder, are children being respected in the same manner? What right does another person have over another, age? The color of your uniform? I think we are all worthy of respect and love for one another.

Dealing with Defeat

In our children's lives there are many times when they will be engaged in a competition of some sort. This is a time when a person's inner shadow seems to present itself. My son and I were watching the Sochi Winter Olympics and afterwards there were evaluations and tryouts for our local baseball team. My son took on a defeated attitude saying things like I'll never make the team, we lost last year. I need to practice every moment until the day of the evaluations. I want it to be perfect. He worked himself up into quite the mood. I sat with him and used the Olympics as a teachable moment. I recalled how we watched many teams/people receive Silver, Gold and Bronze. I explained that there were many people for each event who wouldn't receive any medals. I said each person will handle that in their own way but I will give you two different versions of the same event and I want you to tell me what you learn from each. In one scenario, I said imagine this snowboarder "loses" and falls down in the snow and cries and says I'm such a loser, I suck, I don't want to do any interviews. The second snowboarder also doesn't medal and immediately after hugs his opponents and tells them smiling how great they did, congratulates them and waves to the thousands of people who are there. In his interviews he says, I did my best and I'm proud of myself for just getting here to the Olympics, it just wasn't my time but I look at it this way I'm in a beautiful country I've never been to and I'm going to enjoy and learn from Russian culture and enjoy cheering for the other Olympic events. Now which person do you think has the better attitude and is experiencing joy in life? He said well obviously the second guy. I told him, the second guy was right and that's because the second guy already knows he's a winner before he's done anything. Simply because he exists, he is a winner. You don't have to do anything on the outside to tell you who you are on the inside, you are a beloved and cherished expression of GOD. Is that enough for you? He said, wow Mommy you just changed my whole attitude and I said no you just shifted your awareness from fear to love. No matter how you do in your evaluations Taurean, you are a great thing. The game is a game but you are love. I saw the light return to his eyes and the next day at evaluations he was so calm and did his personal best and was proud of himself. In life we will experience so many different emotions throughout our journey (sometimes all at the same time). Each experience guiding us and showing us something. There are times when fear can save your life and tears to show immense joy or deep pain. Each emotion and the expression of it allows us to really feel our existence. Instead of controlling our emotions and putting them away in a box, our children need to understand that these emotions are a part of us and not a bad thing. The other day for no reason at all I was in a bad mood, and my sister called and knowing me so well could sense it right away. She asked if anything happened and if I was okay I said everything was fine she then proceeded to ignore my bad mood and continue with the conversation. A few hours later the mood had passed and I asked her why she continued to talk and she said because you were fine and I respect that you were in a bad mood and said so. Even though nothing was wrong, you didn't try to fill the space and say well if I'm feeling bad it must be this or that. You were just like I'm in a bad mood and it happens sometimes and it will pass. In positive parenting they may teach children to have only happy thoughts and do things to get rid of bad feelings. Our feelings are there regardless it's our thoughts that determine our attitudes. If you remain calm in your center you can let your emotions come and go like waves in the ocean and not assign events to them and attempt to fill in the blank.

Mindful parenting isn't about a bunch of hard to remember tools and long lists, it's about putting your heart into each moment. I remember reading a book called Love Is Spelled T I M E. I know in today's fast pace society there is never enough time to do the things we really want to do or we can say we'll do this or that with our children tomorrow. Tomorrow comes and goes like a flash of lighting and before we know it, our children have become adults and are virtually strangers because we haven't put any time into the most important thing. I don't spend every waking moment with my son (I think both of us are thankful for that) but the time we do spend together, I try to make it meaningful. We're not always doing something big or engaged in some super important educational lesson. Sometimes we just go outside sit on the porch together and look up at the clouds. Even though we're away from our kids through technology and an old fashioned pen and paper we can let our children know they are never far from our hearts. A heartfelt random text message telling them why you love them or what you love about them can really effect their day. Parents who have older children who may feel distant to them can connect with your children through doing heartfeltl activities together. Creating a family jar titled the Happy Jar and filling it with memories of fun times together can sometimes ease the pain of bad days and situations.

Competition Breeds Contempt

When I think of the word competition, two more words come to mind immediately, winner and losers. No middle man, just one or the other and everyone wants to be the winner. We learn first about competetion in the strangest of places, as new parents. It starts with Janey is talking at 6 mos old, oh but Billy is sleeping through the night at 2 weeks (Top That! I can imagine another Mom thinking). I of course only found out about this comepetition of baby wars after becoming a parent. When my son was infant and other Moms were around the Q & A would begin easily enough, "so is he doing xyz? If your son is you get the look of approval but then it moves into well how old was he when he started doing this? Well my Johnny was (always younger when their prodigy started doing said milestone) x many months. As they become toddlers and then young children the competition continues. My daughter speaks three languages, what does your child do? Some may feel the need to then put their child in something just to say oh well she is teaching classes at Harvard and she's only 5! When our children see and hear us carrying on like this, it tells them that I need to do this or that to be better than my friend and if I am not doing better than my friend then Mom can't brag about me. The child then becomes competitve and eventually picks up where the parents left off.

To offset young children feeling bad about "not winning" an event some activities/sports teams have started giving out trohies to all particpants and naturally the competitive parents are in an uproar and some even go as far as to state, my son isn't getting a trophy because he didn't earn it and not every child is a winner -ouch! I am a recovering former comepetitive person so I hear where the parents are coming from but I see where living in a competitive world has landed humanity as a whole. Countries are comepeting against each other to have the best military weapons, to have the best education system, to have the best economy etc. In all this competing for being the best and being the winner, we as a society have left the actual people behind. In education in the public school system there have been tests at least every two to three months and all a test really assesses is how well a child can memorize information. I personally have a photographic memory so studying was nothing to me, in fact in I just glance at something long enough I will remember it for a test or however long I need to retain the information in my brain but that is not true knowledge if just a few short months later I cannot apply what I have learned. Competing with other schools just for bragging rights is stressful to children who are overwhelmed with the litany of material they are required to learn. I have found that my son is the same as I am, He had been bringing home perfect papers and of course I would do the obligatory great job then months later ask him if he knew thus and so and he would have no idea how to arrive at the answer but he passed or met his benchmarks or whatever test it was and so the teacher was happy but what did he really learn?

If we are busy competing with others, what happens when the others win? We spend valuable time trying to win next time or thinking how they cheated or what have you. It doesn't lead to warm fuzzy feelings for the so called winner. The "loser" may start to dislike the person, country, school that won and that can lead to contempt.

Instead of holding someone in contempt while competing, I wholeheardtedly believe in an altogether different ideology. Instead of competing we should collaborate with others. Instead of saying this is the best school or that is the winning whatever why not look at each thing and see, is there something of value that we can use and apply to our philosophy. This Earth is an abundant one and we are all created uniquely, we can contribute to each others lives in ways we never imagined and grow and learn together. If children were connected to children in other countries, cities and towns and had the chance to just be children and express their ideas and create together, there would be no need to distinguish between what is the best.

One evening while watching television I happened to catch and interesting story about two enormously intelligent inventors, Nikola Tesla and Thomas Edison. One invented alternating current and the other is known for inventing the light bulb among many other talents. They worked together a short while then became arch enemies and began a lifelong competition with trying to "best" the other one. They spent years in court fighting over different patents and ideas all the while losing money fighting the various court battles. Although one of them won their court case by the time he finished paying all the attorney's fees he died almost penniless in a hotel alone. My only take away from the documentary was imagine what those two would have invented had they just collaborated with each other, unfortunately now we will never know.

Parent to Parent

Let's face it, parenting is challenging. It is a constant struggle to juggle everything in our lives as well as our children's lives. Learning different ways of parenting can come from any and everywhere. Leaving yourself open for knowledge can only enrich our already complex lives and lead to a more peaceful existence. One family that I enjoy learning about and using some of their tips is a family that has 19 children, they currently have a documentary television show. The show is about the parents and their children and grandchildren and basically how they connect as a family. While I don't follow all of their practices I do incorporate some of them and have total admiration for the love they show to their children. They teach that parents should praise their children more than scolding and instead of focusing so much on practice makes perfect, they instead teach the more loving approach which is practice makes progress. Watching their show also inspires more patience with myself. When I feel overwhelmed, I think if this family can do this with so many children, surely I am capable of this task as well. Not only do I learn from a few television programs I also read parenting magazines, take advice from friends and teachers. Parenting with love is an open hearted journey that assists us with the necessary tools to bring forth the lights that are children are to let them burst forth and express the goodness that they are.

Bullying

----

*"The saint and the sinner are merely exchanging notes. The saint
has a past the sinner has a future, therefore no need to judge"*
-Deepak Chopra

In recent years this seems to be an ever growing issue. With the
advent of social media, bullying seems to occur not only with children
but adults as well. Teaching our children how to navigate these
uncomfortable encounters will provide them with the necessary
tools to come out unscathed. This is an issue that I know about all
too well. I have experienced bullying from Kindergarten through
college. Growing up and being extremely shy pretty much put a
bull's eye target on my back for being picked on. I've only recently
acquired the necessary perspective to navigate through this issue.
Now that my son is school age, he is starting to be exposed to
such behaviors. One thing that I have taught him is about being
authentic and feeling good about yourself. I explained to him
that only hurt people hurt other people. In the past weeks two
separate incidents have occurred and I used them both as learning
opportunities. In the one incident he was at a Parents Night Out
program and some of the other kids kept pushing him off of a

bench when it was time for dinner. He came home pretty sad and wanted to go back another time and be mean to them. I read a book to him called Have You Filled a Bucket Today? Which explains that each person (and animal) has a bucket that holds their good thoughts and feelings in it. When we do something good we are filling a bucket and when we are mean not only are we dipping from the other person's bucket we are dipping out our bucket also. I explained that the children who were being mean were bucket dippers and that they are ultimately being mean to themselves when they dishonor another child. A few days later at his baseball game, my son is talking to another child (a teammate) in the outfield and the other child kept making fun of my son and the whole team. Taurean kept looking at me and then yelled really loud you are teasing me and I don't like it, stop! I looked to the boy's parents for help but found them laughing about their son's behavior. When Taurean's team was up to bat I came to the fence of the dugout and whispered in his ear, that child was being a bucket dipper but remember he dipped from his own bucket too. It happened to be this child's turn to bat and although he usually is a great hitter this time he was struck out swinging, which made him cry coming back to the dugout. Instead of my son making fun of this child back, he walked over and said that's okay you will hit it next time. The child looked confused as I'm sure he expected to be teased as well. For the rest of the game this child was nice to the team and when the game was over and we were walking across the parking lot we hear someone yelling, Bye Taurean! Taurean didn't want to say good-bye back to him but I said we don't carry grudges okay and you show him that. He said he was really being mean at the beginning.

I said but once you showed him kindness his behavior changed so we can't keep responding to his negative behavior and it's not there anymore. Taurean's grandmother chimed in and said, maybe that guy was only mean because he didn't know what else to say but he wanted to make friends with you guys. So maybe at the next game you should try talking to him.

It seems that everyone on the surface is anti-bullying and schools adopt special colors and take a stand against it yet every other month or so we keep hearing stories of children being bullied. The solution seems to be for the bullied child to speak to an adult or trusted friend about the bullying however the real issue for me is the child who is doing the bullying. Yes we want our children to not be bullied but we have to ask ourselves what is making this child (the bully) come to this decision to hurt another one. My sister's boss' son had a bullying incident that occurred on a school bus that went viral. The child being of a different culture dressed in their native attire and was teased relentlessly on the school bus for it day after day. The child was so frustrated and upset that they pulled out their phone and videotaped the bullying. The video while deeply troubling for the child being bullied also made me think why would another child do this, to that extent. Obviously both children are going through something and both need help.

Compassion

Compassion means to suffer with another, essentially to feel their heart with yours. There are often times when I am out attending an event and I'll see a Mom with several children, and one of them cying and another running off. I also witness other mothers making comments about how they never let their children act out and she doesn't know what she is doing. Instead of passing judgment, offer her compassion. Feeling with someone makes human. It's easy to go out into society and label this one as a bad parent or her children are bad. Parents (myself included) also have trouble asking for help, we think if we ask for help it means admitting we can't do it all. Parenting is a joyful, strange, and complicated journey that we take on.

Building self-confidence

We all want the best for our children and we want them to experience the most that life has to offer and to follow their passion and live with a purpose. The best way for children to succeed in life is to live from the inside out. Building our children up and giving them praise and understanding as they navigate different scenarios in life is a contributing factor to their confidence. If we constantly tell them they are doing a good job and cheerleading them, they learn to seek fulfillment outside of themselves and will always require that outside stimuli to make them feel worthy. Assisting them to build their own self confidence will have life lasting effects.

When my son has done something or acquired a new skill, I will ask him how does it feel to know that you did that yourself or how does he feel about himself? Then whatever he is feeling we will explore that subject deeper. I always tell him, it's not important how I think you did, it's important how you think and feel that you did. To start children out building their self-esteem early doesn't have to be a series of complicated learning techniques or a lot of knowledge they don't yet possess. It can be something as simple as coming up with your own song. My son and I created *The Affirmation Song*. We sing this song pretty often and the nice thing is that the lyrics aren't set in stone and we change the lyrics to the mood of the day. He stands on his bed in the morning and looks in his mirror and sings I am Happy, I am kind, I can do most anything, I am healthy I am calm I can do most anything. To delve deeper with older children to make sure they are aware of what they are singing you can then say what does happy feel like inside, what are some ways that you can be kind today as we go out into the world.

When my son started having seizures he had to go to the hospital often and see a multitude of doctors. Some things changed in his everyday life and I began to see it affecting his self-confidence and it was painful to see him go through feelings of doubting himself and his abilities. I created a book for him with positive affirmations and a picture to represent the affirmation. On one page the affirmation is I am creative and under is a picture of a series of projects that he has created. Another one states I am a winner and it's a picture of his 1st place ribbon he received for giving an oral presentation. I made the book and didn't really say anything to him about, I just slipped it in his book bag one morning. A week went by and he hadn't mentioned it to me and I thought perhaps he didn't see the book in there yet but I still didn't bring it up. So one evening he was doing his homework at the dining room table and became frustrated and exclaimed I can'- doesn't finish the statement but instead runs to his backpack and pulls the book out opens to a page and said I can do this, I can do anything I set my mind to, see Mommy! Then he proceedsed to figure out how to solve the problem and moved on. I said, did you find that book today in your backpack? He exuberantly replied are you crazy I've had this book for weeks and I look at it every day this is the best book ever thank you! Whenever I don't understand something or I feel bad about myself I open my book and I know who I am. Although I was elated that this book was helping him I still wanted to be sure that he is aware of his gifts and talents on his own without any input from me. Thankfully I saw evidence of that a few weeks later when he came in from school excitedly telling me he had something to show me. In the book I of affirmations I had wrote for him he went on and added his own and he said there are so many things about myself that are great I may need more paper!

Co-parenting

It takes a village to raise a child is indeed a true statement. From the time our children first enter the world they are surrounded by people who will influence their lives either by direct interaction with them or witnessing the effects of their parents interactions with them. Raising children requires love and communication. Communication between parents shows children how to be in their relationships. There are times when parents will have fights and cause disharmony in their environment. Understanding how to have a disagreement without attacking a person's character helps separate the person from the action.

I became a single parent to my son when he was still an infant and although the divorce occurred when he became a toddler I still explained that it happened. Burying painful events and refusing to talk about them will only make children more curious. When I initially went through the divorce it was extremely difficult for me to process and did require a time of absence from my ex-husband. We are in a unique position as we live several states away from each other. Our love for our son unites us through many obstacles and helped us to overcome them. My Ex-husband resides near my home state so I always make time for my son and Ex-husband to get together. In addition to that my Ex-husband had the brilliant idea of handwriting letters to my son. My son just loves running down to the mailbox and getting a letter addressed to him. Now that he is older, he is able to write letters back to him and gets so much enjoyment running down to the mailbox and lifting the red flag to signal to the postman we have an outgoing letter. We even turned it into an adventure when we walked down to the mailbox one day to put a letter in and discovered we had locked ourselves out of the house! It is really beautiful to experience him develop a wonderful loving relationship with his father. Of course his father and I have made mistakes but we always promote the other parent. I always tell him Daddy is doing a great job and doing his best and loves him very much. My Ex-husband always tells my son Mommy is a great Mommy and loves you very much and you should listen to what she says because she has your best interest in mind. Your Mom is the best! In addition to the letters they write they also Skype a few times a week. Initially I sat there to assist my son with the computer but now that he is more comfortable I will set him up and sit off in another room so they can create a sense of "their time" together. It really works out when my son has painted something that day or invented a new song or whatever he can show it to Daddy immediately and they can have a live discussion on it. There were things that occurred in my marriage that were less than favorable and some friends and family members were witness to it, despite their opinions no one is allowed to dishonor my Ex-husband in anyway in my son's presence. Constantly berating the other parent, whether it's done by a parent or close relatives can create a damaging effect on the child. Children have an innate ability to internalize everything they see and hear. When parents go through a divorce or break up it doesn't mean an end to their relationship with the other parent. I try to be as honest as I can with my son about what happened and take personal responsibility. When he is older I will go more in depth.

Talking about different things that may shift in family dynamics is key. When my son's Paternal grandmother passed away he was only two years old, it was devastating for all of us. I knew as he got older his memories of her would fade and eventually he would only remember stories of her. I make sure to tell him that his other Gaga (the name he came up with to call his grandmothers) is still with him and loves him very much. A few months after she had passed we decided to plant flowers on her birthday we found roses that matched the color of her favorite fingernail polish. Every year they bloom on her birthday and I remind him about her. Although she wasn't my mother she was an integral part of my son's life and family and it is important to honor her memory.

As I stated earlier, it takes a village to bring up these beautiful souls entrusted to us. In the times when people lived together in wilderness communities each woman looked out for the others child. The eldest people in the tribes were thought to possess the most wisdom. Unfortunately some of us may find that we are living states or countries away from our "village" and feel the task of parent is solely left to us the parents. I believe we can create our own sense of village throughout our lives with the people we meet along the way. When my son started having his seizures, there were initially many visits to the local childrens's hospital. During one particular visit a doctor entered the room glanced around at the people in my son's room and asked, Ok, so how is everyone related to the patient? A hush fell over the room that had only moments before been filled with chatter. We all looked from one to another, not quite sure what to say until finally someone said "we're all family". On one side of my son's bed was my half -brother's Mom who coincidently worked at the hospital. Next to her sat my former step-dad as he and my Mom had divorced 12 years earlier but had remained great friends. My Mom and I sat on the other side of my son's bed holding his hand and patting his head. For the first time I realized how this may appear to be an odd assortment of people gathered at my son's bedside. But these are just some of the people in our village that we have created away from home. My Mom and my brother's Mom get along very well and my son has stayed at her house numerous times. My step-dad doesn't live in our state but has remained a constant in our lives over the years.

Labeling

Labels were created to give us a short synopsis of a product or experience without wasting too much time or energy figuring out what something is. In some instances when something has a label we are thankful however labeling when it comes to our children can set them up for self-limiting beliefs or keep them trapped in a box. As a child I myself was labeled as the shy, good girl who was perfect. I felt this word shy constantly haunting me at times. As a young adult I was so shy that I was too intimidated to enter into a regular store alone. This belief was placed upon me from an early age and unconsciously I kept renewing that subscription of myself. This goes back to an earlier comment I made when I am out amongst crowds of people or friends and they say, my son is bad or they are always up to no good. Labeling helps in all areas except where people are concerned. It teaches us to dehumanize the person we are labeling and then opens up a space to dishonor them. I unknowingly became a part of another labeling theory by my 5th grade teacher Mrs. White. Now although I never met my 5th grade teacher prior to 5th grade she decided to label me as she would put it L.A.Z.Y. on the first day of class. When I told her I wanted to sing she laughed in my face so I stopped trying out in talent shows and quit the choir and when I expressed an interest in writing again she scoffed and said I was too L.A.Z.Y. and didn't know how to correctly use then and than in a sentence so I would never write a book. I told her I wanted to be the next Jackie Joyner Kersey and she told me I was too slow. Eventually Mrs. White's voice became my own voice and for years I woke up and told myself the things she had expressed to me. It's taken a lot of soul work to understand and move through my experiences and to release that negative energy and no longer claim it as my own voice. I don't tell this story as a woe is me narrative. I am sharing in hopes that it can prevent your child from unfairly being labeled by someone whose opinion doesn't matter in their journey of life. As parents we should be aware that not all labeling comes from peers or bullies sometimes the culprit is the one we've entrusted our children to or ourselves. I don't hold any ill feelings toward Mrs. White or any of her actions, I understand now as an adult that she was on her own journey in life and was doing her best in her eyes. Had she known the internal impact it had on my life, I choose to think she would've chosen another path. When we label ourselves and each other we then unconsciously submit to that word or idea that has been placed upon us instead of simply being. Interestingly enough now I take the shy label that I grew up with and turned it into a conversation starter. My normal M.O. is to try to blend in with a crowd or group by saying as little as possible and then silently berate myself for not saying anything or being more outgoing. Now when I am approaching a social situation I address it head on. I'll say I am kind of shy initially when I meet people but then I warm up and become a blabber mouth. Somehow just saying that statement takes the pressure off and relaxes me. Learning this technique has come in handy when parenting a child whose personality is extremely different from my own.

Parenting Your Opposite

As I've mentioned before labeling can be detrimental to a person's overall development. Especially when a parent will say something to the effect of my son is such a sissy he is nothing like I was as a boy or my daughter is into trucks and bugs but I was a dainty princess as a little girl. Our children are not clones of us and should not be held to any standards of what we did as children. My son is as different from me as North and South. As a child I was afraid to speak to anyone especially strangers and my son never meets a stranger. I approached the world from a place of fear whereas his approach is that everyone is here to love me and be loved by me and they are so eager to hear what I have to say. Although socially this is something I have struggled with in the past, I don't place upon him my fears or experiences as a child. He is free to be himself in whatever form he wishes to express himself. A person who maneuver's well through social interactions may find a child who doesn't easily connect with others to be painstaking. Instead of pushing your child to be more like you, use this as a learning experience for you to learn a different personality type and understand their perspective. Although our children are sent here to learn from us, we often end up learning more from them than we think.

Religion/Spiritual practice

This may be a controversial issue for many people but if you keep an open heart and mind perhaps we may learn to look at things in a new light or find an appreciation for that which already resonates within you. My upbringing was based in Baptist Christianity. From the time I was three years old I attended church with my great-grandparents every Sunday and I also was on the choir (which only consisted of myself and two other cousins my same age) and later attended Bible study. As a young child the concept of Jesus was introduced to me and I loved him. I often had dreams that at night my spirit went to Jesus and I would sit with him and tell him about my day. This happened until I was a teenager and was then introduced to the idea of God who records all your wrongs and is waiting until you die to judge you. Toward the end of my late teen years I became obsessed with Buddha and learning about enlightenment and reincarnation. As a young adult I became over come with a fear of God or anything associated with God. I felt I was damned to hell because I was taught that if you think a bad thought you are damned and it's just as if you committed the act anyway. Though I acknowledged the divine presence I was fearful of its intimacy because of my sinful thinking. Once I became a parent though, it opened my heart to a more loving and accepting

GOD. I read a book by Marianne Williamson called A Return to Love which is based on A Course in Miracles which led me to my own personal truth. After reading that book and conducting research I began to see that most of what we as people believe is told to us when we are children. Some of these viewpoints are accepted and never questioned or truly thought about. I have a friend who practices a different faith and once when asked why things were done in a certain way, she had no idea why she performed the ritual but that her parents did it so she does. When questioned furthered she concluded she isn't really sure what she believes because she just accepted what was taught to her and never pondered it for herself.

In deciding what to teach my son about faith, religion and spirituality I wanted him to be the deciding factor of his faith. I feel it is my responsibility to share with him the various beliefs that exist. With my child, instead of forcing him to believe what I believe, I allow him the freedom to ask questions about God and to state his true beliefs. I expose him to many different religions, (Christianity, Hinduism, Muslim, Seeks, Buddhists and atheists) and practices so he can make an informed decision for himself. Learning about other religions also teaches him to respect other people's religious principles although they may be different from his. Becoming a parent helped me to see that the God I choose to believe in is not sitting on a cloud looking down with disapproving fingers pointing at all of us. I am very careful to state when teaching him that this is what I personally believe or this is what this religion believes; it lets him know that he is free to choose what is true for him. My personal belief is that there are many paths to the same destination, while one specific path will resonate with one (ex: Christianity) yet another may resonate with someone else (agnosticism). Oftentimes I hear people talking about GOD's wrath and judgment and fearing him/her yet sometimes I wonder if we as humans have placed our small minded limited beliefs onto GOD.

Mom-tuition

We've all heard the phrase trust your gut or listen to your intuition. I think for women when we become mother's our intuition kicks in to an even higher gear so that we have another tool to assist us in navigating through this role. The motto I use in regards to my son in when in doubt trust your heart. This next story is something I am still very much dealing with and don't have answers for and is near and dear to my heart.

December 11 I woke in the middle of the night to agonizing sounds coming from my son's bedroom. I ran to his room still half asleep and found him on his floor a little disoriented and hysterical. After calming him down I asked him what happened, he told me he woke up and couldn't walk and was trying to drag himself to his bedroom door. I tried to stand him up and his legs gave out and he flopped to the floor. Since this had never occurred I didn't know where exactly to put this incident in my mind though on some other level it deeply disturbed me. I contacted his pediatrician who was perplexed as well. He went in to see the doctor and they ran some tests and everything appeared fine. December 21 I am again woken to the hysterical sounds of my son screaming and he seems visibly shaken by something and can't walk. Within a few minutes the feeling returns to his leg and he goes back to sleep. Two days later it happened again, this time I took him to a Children's Hospital where they said he was more than likely experiencing night terrors along with growing pains. They ran a few tests and sent us home. At the follow up visit to his pediatrician she read the notes from the hospital and the note stated that my son was refusing to walk due to growing pains in his legs at night. To me something just didn't add up. Cut to a few months later, I am up late one night wondering what had made my son look so strange and then not have the ability to walk. In the pit of my stomach I had the feeling that there was more to the story. An hour after I had that feeling, I was awakened to the sound of my son hysterically screaming and not being able to walk again. This time, since I had those earlier thoughts/feelings I decided to bring him into my room although he had calmed down and was ready to get back to sleep. He fell asleep easily and eventually I did as well. The next time I woke up it was because I had been hit in the back really hard. When I turned around to move my son away from me I saw that his arms were convulsing and so were his legs. His eyes initially had a vacant stare and then began rolling around in his head which was also shaking violently. I was witnessing a seizure for the first time. I had no idea what to do and panicked for the first few minutes. I called for my Mom figuring she may know what to do. During that week he had more seizures and we spent a lot of time at the children's hospital and back and forth to the pediatrician. As I stated earlier this is still unfolding and I am in the process of learning a lot about what is happening or could be happening to my son. Sometimes I wonder what would've happened if I hadn't decided to bring him into my room. It was just a nagging sensation that I was missing something. I would have never witnessed the seizures because I now know that he is asleep when they occur and only wakes up afterwards. Sometimes if he is near the edge of the bed when the seizure starts he will end up on the floor and temporary paralysis is a common side effect of his type seizures. When I looked at pieces of the puzzle it just didn't make sense why he wouldn't remember how he had come to be on the floor and why he couldn't walk.

I want to urge all parents to pay attention to that still small voice that is there guiding us. Also if you notice your child screaming out in the middle of the night you may want to keep an eye on them, it could be more than just a nightmare or night terrors. The screaming my son does isn't ordinary I'm upset screaming or crying, this is the hysterical almost inconsolable screaming. Throughout the times that my son has had seizures I have had to use rescue medication and I shudder to think if he had one of those seizures in a room alone and I was completely unaware that he was having them.

Since my son has started having seizures he is now on different medicines and some of them are adult sized pills. When I picked up the prescription for one particular medicine I observed that they were adult sized pills to be split in half and given once a day. Initially I asked the pharmacist and his doctor if he could have a liquid prescription. After they declined to change it I came home and loosely cut up a pill and snuck it into some food. I then sat there intensely watching my son to make sure he didn't notice that his food tasted slightly different and also making sure he ate all of it. The next day the next dosage was to be given and I couldn't figure out which food to put it in. After scanning the pantry and fridge for a few seconds I landed on the oatmeal. I crushed up his medicine and cleverly stirred the oatmeal making sure all the medicine was concealed and then handed him the bowl and literally sat in his face and urged him to eat the oatmeal. A short while later he looked at me inquisitively and asked Mom, why do you want me to eat this so bad? I sat there silent for a minute trying to think of a way to trick him into eating it and then I thought, just be honest. I replied well bud, your medicine is in the oatmeal. Remember we picked up that prescription the other day? Well this medicine is grownup medicine and you can't take all of it so Mommy has to crush some of it up and put it in something that you eat. His response made me feel wonderful about being honest with him. He nonchalantly said, cool, can I crush up the pill next time and put it in my food? I was truly amazed on one hand and not surprised on the other.

As caretakers and guardians of our children we often think of our children as not being able to handle the truth. That is a mistake, children on the contrary are much more resilient than we can imagine. When my son first had his seizure I whispered the word or talked in a different room but I came to the realization that this is a part of his life and knowledge is power. So I sat him down and told him what was going on with his body, we looked up some things on the internet and helped him to feel comfortable with life. When he heard that he would have to have and MRI the doctor described it to him, he seemed scared. Since he is really into space I told him, when you get your MRI you're actually going in to a space shuttle for one. You will get to feel exactly what astronauts feel when they are going into space. It then became something that he looked forward to.

Now almost two years into his seizure diagnosis my son struggles with how it affects his life and some of his limitations. There are time when weeks fly by without any seizure activity and then some weeks he will have them every day for a period of time. When they occur frequently he becomes terrified of going to sleep (he only has nocturnal seizures). He will look at me pleadingly and asks the question that I dread, "Mommy will I have a seizure tonight? It is such a loaded question for me as it is a reminder that our lives have changed and taken unforeseen twists and turns. I would love nothing more than to guarantee my child a peaceful night of rest with wonderful dreams but I can't. Instead I offer him the only I have to give, myself. I tell him," I don't know if you will have any seizures tonight but I can promise you that if you do, I am right here with you and once the seizure has passed I will hug you and hold you and we will get through it together one breath at a time.

Sometimes in the unpleasantness of life we find blessings along the way to open our eyes and heal our hearts. My son's seizures have allowed me to find the gratitude in the smallest of things. I used to get irritated that my son always runs everywhere and jumps and climbs or karate chops but after witnessing times when he can't move any part of his body I am thankful for the days of non-stop running and jumping.

As parents we have a natural desire to protect our babies from the difficulties and sadness of the world. Thankfully life gives us opportunities to learn and grow through life's obstacles and to live life with grace. I sometimes have a tendency to fall into a woe is me attitude when something unexpected occurs but then I tell myself this is just an opportunity for my heart to understand something and a new way for my compassion to expand. Then I focus on what I am grateful for. No matter what we go through as parents we must always trust and have faith that we will make it through whatever comes our way.

Listen and Make the Connection

"You will find as you look back upon your life that the moments when you have truly lived are the moments when you have done things in the spirit of love."
-Henry Drummond

If there was one thing that I had to say was the most important, it would be that we listen to our children. Instead of barking orders or laying down the law come to your child with an open heart ready to listen to their thoughts and feelings on a subject. Fully listening with our hearts, ears and eye contact gives the child assurance that you are truly interested in what they have to say. I know life can get hectic and it may seem that there isn't time to fully listen as most of us are multi-tasking many things at one.

While scrolling through my facebook page one day I came across a post that a Mom had written about her child. Her son was 11 at the time to which she posted something to the effect of my son is so hard headed and difficult to talk to to, I beat him so much and he still does the same thing. I told him if he does X again I am giving up on him. I mean it, I will be done with him for good. My heart ached for the Mom and son in this situation. Over and over people commented asking her not to give up on her child to which she replied that her son won't tell her anything and has always been like that. It made me think about my relationship with my son (who was only a toddler at the time) and wonder is this where our relationship could be headed in the future. Then I thought how things were between us. I have made it a point to always communicate with my son and talk to him about his interests and concerns. I always tell him that he can be honest with me because we have a judgment free zone. I also find a space to share things about my childhood to let him see things from a different perspective. If as parents we leave a space for honesty and compassion, our children will confide in us. Once you have established a connection and safe space for sharing thoughts, feelings and emotions we should work to maintain that connection. I know sometimes as parents we may want to seem as though we have it all together. Showing children a perfect parent but living something else, creates a disconnect. Being authentic in your approach allows space for mistakes on both parties.

My son started a new school and a week into the school year, his teacher sent home his papers and they had either 0's or 2's and his teacher also called very concerned about his performance. I was quite puzzled as I had homeschooled him for the previous 2 years so I knew he had learned this material. When he came home from school I didn't' lecture him or scream at him. I simply asked; hey bud what's going on at school these days? He said well Mom, as you know I prefer to be at home with you teaching me and so don't tell anyone but I came up with this plan. I figure if I pretend to do bad in school you will think this school isn't teaching me anything and then you will withdraw me. I hadn't taken into account how transitioning to a brick and mortar school would affect my son and was concerned with my grownup obligations. Once I realized this was a period of adjustment for all of us and informed his teachers, his experience slowly changed.

When our children get home from school as parents we are curious as to how their day went and what they learned about. If your children are like most, then their answer is a grunt or it was okay. After getting a lot of okay I employed a technique that a friend of mine uses. You take a mason jar or really anything you may have around the house, think of questions that engage your child or create avenues to open up the lines of communication. Once they start talking they eventually get around to what really happened at school. While we are at work and they are at school/daycare babysitter or away from us, we can still keep that connection going by leaving a note in their lunch box or during the year going to their school to have lunch with them.

One of the most meaningful ways I believe to connect with our children is to read to/with them. Of all my childhood memories, this is one that stood out the most for me. Growing up my Mom worked long hours so we rarely saw her during the week however no matter what she always made it a priority to read to us each night from the Bible book for Children. It wasn't so much what she was reading but the gift of her full presence with us each night before bed.

The first thing I ever bought for my child long before he was born was a book of children's stories. Reading to him was one practice I knew without a doubt that would be a part of our journey together.

I know that reading to them every night can seem like a somewhat daunting task at times. A lot of times we are operating off of little to no sleep, the laundry has piled up and the dinner dishes are still in the sink but if you can spare just 10-15 minutes a night with your children, it will make a world of difference. I remember a time when my son wanted the same book read to him every night for an entire year (unfortunately for me though that story has been relegated to my long term memory), or he picked out a story to read that was incredibly long (never read Mike Mulligan and Marianne when you are trying to get through story time quickly). Reading to them when they are little not only exposes them to new ideas and concepts but also encourages them to foster their own imagination. When children are ready to start reading it helps them feel more confident. When reading is an interactive activity between the family it creates a sacred space for family time. Now my son loves to read and even though he does it on his own, I still read to him at bed time. We have taken it a step farther now and he writes his own little books if he wants a book on a particular topic and it doesn't exist or we can't find it.

On Death and Dying

I have been thinking about this subject for a while. One day I drove to the church parking lot where my son plays softball. He plays for a church league, the field which has three different fields for each level is on one side then there is a small road and a makeshift parking lot field that is essentially the same space as the cemetery. One particularly beautiful Saturday morning, you know the kind where the sky is so blue, the morning air has that unmistakable crispness to it. The smell of grilled hamburgers and hot dogs makes your stomach churn as the scent tickles your nostrils. As I pulled in to the parking lot, I saw a tent and a casket surrounded by mourners. They were dressed in black, heads bent in silence. I got out the car and heard the laughter and shouts from the baseball fields. I looked to my left and saw parents, family and friends cheering on their teams and looked to my right to saw the funeral. I looked up at the beautiful sky and thought that is so awful for those people mourning their loved one. Then I thought, wait isn't that what life is all about. Living in the present while we're here and isn't death a reminder for us to live. Those sweet souls on the baseball field probably never felt more alive than being in the throes of their games, running bases and stopping runs. We all know this is but a moment that we spend on Earth. Inevitably we will all travel that same road someday. Instead of feeling sorrowful, I felt grateful that I was alive. I said a prayer over the one who left Earth and for their family members. Then I walked toward the field and took a deep breath and just before I stepped into the field area I looked around and imprinted the scene upon my heart. The sky was a cotton candy blue with thin streaks of white here and there. The wind blew ever so slightly, not enough to blow the dirt in your eyes but just enough so that it felt as though the wind was gently caressing your skin and saying all is well. The lovely smells of grilled burgers and hot dogs filled the air along with the scent of wild honeysuckle growing nearby. I can't recall which team won that day however I do vividly remember feeling so alive with love, and excitement that it was truly a transcendent moment for me.

Children will inevitably experience the loss of family members and friends throughout their lives and it is up to us to assist them with this delicate situation. More than likely children will experience the death of their grandparents first as was the case with me. I was 8 years old when my great grandmother passed away. She was the kind of woman that is almost extinct in today's fast paced technology world. I never saw her without an apron on. She grew all of her own food, and then canned the food for the winter. By trade she was a hair dresser but to me she appeared to be a master of all things. Whenever there was a birthday in the family she made the birthday cake completely from scratch. I liked Strawberry Shortcake (the cartoon figure) so I would get an actual cake in the shape of strawberry shortcake. She sewed her own clothes, made everything from scratch, had a garden and had a gentle overall nature. Her and my grandfather had a camper and would travel all over during the summer months and sometimes take us great grans with them. When I stayed weekends with my grandparents we would sit in the mornings and have coffee (this was the late 80's) and grits together. I say all this to say that I had a close relationship with my great grandmother. When I found out she had passed away, it was overhearing a conversation between my mom, grandmom and great grandpop. I was never formally told, and when I asked to attend the funeral it was out of the question. The day of the funeral I remember feeling awful inside and wishing I could see her one last time and say good bye. Then I wanted to talk about it with the grown-ups around me but no one gave me that outlet. I overheard my Mom telling her best friend that we were too young to be burdened with death so she wanted to shield us from that. But life has its own ideas for us. Two years later one of my classmates Stephanie was hit by a car and killed crossing the highway and a place where my friends and I used to also cross all the time. It was decided that all the children from our two elementary classes would attend the funeral, although it was summer. After the funeral we convened at another classmate's house where we had the opportunity to discuss our emotions and feelings about Stephanie passing. Though I didn't yet possess the vocabulary to articulately express the fullness of the loss, the process of being allowed to speak aided in my understanding of the moment and assisted in my healing process. I went home and wrote down my thoughts and feelings. The process of writing your feelings down about such a terrible situation allows you to mentally process what has occurred.

In 2006 Steve Irwin (nicknamed the Crocodile Hunter) was fatally stung in the heart by a stingray. Prior to his death he had traveled the world informing people about animals of all kinds and teaching us to treat them kind. Steve approached his life and love of animals with enthusiasm and passion. The fascinating aspect of Steve Irwin was his daughter Bindi Irwin. During his memorial service at just 8 years old his daughter addressed a crowd of thousands to talk about her Daddy in a letter she had written. In it she said "My father was my hero-he was always there for me when I needed him. He listened to me and taught me so many things, but most of all he was fun. I know that Daddy had an important job. He was working to change the world so that everyone would love wildlife like he did. He built a hospital to help animals and he bought lots of land to give animals a safe place to live. He took me and my brother and my Mum with him all the time. We filmed together, caught crocodiles together and loved being in the bush together. I don't want Daddy's passion to ever end. I want to help endangered wildlife just like he did. I have the best Daddy in the whole world and I will miss him every day. When I see a crocodile I will always think of him and I know that Daddy made this zoo so everyone could come and learn to love all the animals. Daddy made this place his whole life and now it's our turn to help Daddy"

Earlier I mentioned that one day our children and our children's children will be the only proof that we ever existed and that our children are living legacies of all that is possible in the world. Steve Irwin may not have used the exact words "mindful parenting" or "conscious parenting" but it is evident in the way his daughter has honored and continues to honor him.

Children are so much more present than adults as children their brains can grasp ideas like a sponge and build from them. If we teach them that death is something we should try to avoid at all costs, that isn't equipping them with the tools necessary to embody the fullness of what they will experience.

The word death has such a negative connotation that I was hesitant to include this subject, then realized that is exactly what we do in life. Death happens all the time, everyday but we just aren't discussing it. Buddhist Monk Thich Nhat Hanh uses a comparison on our interpretation for birth and death using a piece of paper. "if we are to look at a piece of paper deeply, we can see the paper is made from trees, sunshine, water, earth and clouds. Can we say that the tree that made this paper is dead? And when the paper is burned and the ashes float up into the sky have they really died or rather just transformed." Our lives can be viewed in this same way. Whether we tell our children that our loved one is now our special angel or we visit their gravesite, it is important to give a child the avenue to express the feelings of loss they have.

A friend that I grew up with lost her Husband when a drunk driver lost control of his vehicle. Instead of being bitter or angry at having to raise three children alone without the company of her best friend and soul mate she has practiced constant gratitude. She uses her Husband's previous Facebook page to post letters to him about how thankful she is that they built this beautiful life together and how she needs him but knows they will meet again. For her children to cope, she has given them the space to create a Letter's to Daddy Box which includes their letters, paintings and special trinkets they make for him. Although it's only been a few short months she and her children have honored the loss through continuing to live their lives and learning to smile, through eyes of gratitude.

Death doesn't have to be some weird or strange thing that sneaks up on us and then leaves us writhing in fear. Transitioning to the next realm is a natural process that occurs for every one of us. So instead of spending our lives dreading the moment we should try to live each moment fully and by walking our talk, shows our children how to handle it when they experience loss.

What You Say Matters

- -

I think back to one day when I heard loud noises outside my otherwise quiet neighborhood. When I looked out the window I saw my neighbor across the street yelling at his 14 year old daughter, being nosey I walked to the mailbox and as I'm walking I could hear him telling her how stupid she was and how he could play basketball so much better than her and encouraging her to quit. I walked back into my house said a prayer for that girl and eventually moved on and forgot about it. About an hour later I went to the front of my house where I heard the same noise, I thought he couldn't possibly still be yelling at her. I lifted my window and listened and sure enough now he had gone back to her years as a young child saying how she was born stupid and it took her longer than the other children to learn how to ride a bike, and she still sucked at that. His daughter never said one thing back to her father, the entire time she stood there looking him in the eyes while he repeatedly broke her spirit. I felt helpless as I was afraid to step in to an altercation with her father. I can't imagine what she was feeling that day and no doubt there were more days to follow. Around this same time I happened to come across a movie that discusses the effects of our words and an experiment that was conducted on water crystals.

In the 1990's Dr. Masaru Emoto conducted an experiment on the power of prayer, words and intentions. In his experiment he froze water and then analyzed its molecular structure. He primarily used pure water to aid in this experiment. For one sample of water he played music, said prayers, held good thoughts for it and said good pleasantries. To the other sample of water it was told negative things. Throughout each phase of the experiment Dr. Emoto allowed photographers not associated with the experiment to photograph the process. The photographs revealed that the water spoken kindly to and prayed over formed stunning unique crystals, while the water that was spoken to negatively formed disfigured crystals and was often a slightly different color. After learning of this experiment I took it a step farther and thought back to the young girl I had witnessed being berated by her father, I have no doubt that if she were water her crystals would've been disfigured. Some of you may be thinking, what does this have to do with people? Well ultimately it has everything to do with people since around 70% of the human body is composed of water. Now while this experiment is quite unique in that a doctor performed it in a lab with the use of microscopes, freezers and other scientist, the principal of this experiment is something that we ourselves can repeat and use this knowledge to speak love into our children. For fun you can repeat this same experiment with your children using apples. Take one apple cut it in half and place them both in a plastic sandwich baggie for seven days. Take one apple and say only kind things to it and take the second apple and say only negative things to it and record the results. My son conducted this same experiment with an apple for a science project. More than anything this experiment helped him to see the importance of words and the impact they have. The first day he spoke kind words over the "good" apple and then negative words to the "bad" apple. After he spoke to the bad apple he was very sad and wanted to apologize to the apple and felt bad for it. I explained to him that when we use our words as weapons they wound us on the inside and on the outside as well. As the experiment continued my son found it increasingly difficult to be mean to the "bad" apple. This is really an excellent way to teach our children empathy and to not bully other children and to be mindful of what they say. One evening while hanging out with his grandmother my son said some things to his grandmother that weren't so kind. I found out the next day when my Mom called to tell me. I had planned on discussing it with my son that day when he came in from school; however once he arrived home we got into our afternoon routine of homework and checking in with each other and it slipped my mind for the time being. So after dinner and a bath, my son was talking to me then all of sudden puts his finger up and said, "excuse me, I need to call my Gaga I need to go apologize for something. I played coy and asked, what happened that makes you feel like you need to apologize for something? He said, "Well, when me and Gaga were looking up meditations, I became angry for some reason and I said that Gaga never keeps her word to me and she promises me things and never keeps it, I said she doesn't really love me and I thought about Gaga all day at school. I know those things I said to her aren't true and I'm really sorry I said them. So can I talk to her? I allowed to him call her to say he was sorry to her and once he went to bed, his grandmother talked to me and asked if I made him apologize to her. I told her no, he brought it up to me in the middle of talking about something else altogether and I never told him that I knew about yesterday, so his apology is from him searching his own heart and soul.

Meditation: The Sacred Silence

Teaching our children stillness and silence is a vital coping mechanism in teaching them to self-regulate and self-care. Meditation has been around for ages and it is used in various cultures and been proven to positively impact a person's life. It can lower stress levels and reduce anxiety in our overscheduled lives.

As an adolescent I happened into meditation quite by accident. I remember I used to get these terrible head aches and I would take over the counter medicine yet the headache remained and sometimes lasted all day. One day I had one of these mind blowing headaches so I lay on the floor of my bedroom and listened to a tape by a band called Oasis, at the end of one of their tapes was a long instrumental. I laid on the floor thinking for a while and then it seems as though no thought passed through my mind and I'm wasn't sure how much time had passed but I knew I wasn't asleep. I remember feeling after a certain time that the headache had passed. From that moment on whenever I had those headaches I would lie on the floor listen to Oasis and zone out and in an hour or so feel great and return to my day. It wasn't until a few years later in high school while learning about the Buddha that I realized what I had been doing all that time was meditation.

A lot of people think meditation is hard to do or time consuming. One of the major complaints I hear is "I can't turn my mind off" or it's boring. There are multiple ways to meditate and probably one that suits your personality and that of your child.

For small children it may be difficult to get them to sit quietly for an extended period of time. In that instance children can learn to do a walking meditation, because they have lots of energy and like to move around this allows them the movement they need but also creates a space for their thoughts to become still by quietly moving. In a walking meditation, you can take them outside and just walk quietly for five minutes. If that doesn't sound appealing there is a 15 minutes meditation in which for the first 5 minutes allows your children to run, jump, skip or any sort of high energy movement then have them speak gibberish for 5 minutes. When we speak in a language unknown it allows our brains to quiet down. For the last 5 minutes have them lie down and play and just breathe. If neither of those options seem appealing then you can always find meditations through a search engine. My son and I practice meditations and when he was really into robots he asked for a robot meditation to which I said, Baby, I'm sure there is no such thing as a robot meditation" however I typed it into a website and sure enough there existed a robot meditation. There are guided meditations in which a person guides a child through a meditation and into sleep, you yourself can guide your child through meditation. One day I was playing around and started to guide my son through one just mimicking how I think they sound and to my surprise my son said wow Mommy I think I enjoy your meditations can you do another one. I have also incorporated meditation into my son's post seizure response. When he comes out of seizures he is hysterical, frantic and his breathing is quick and panicked. So I will lay behind him and gently whisper for him to breathe in slowly and to breathe out and to remember he has the power to control his breathing. Meditation is not always about being in a quiet peaceful place because sometimes that isn't possible. Meditation is about keeping a quiet center inside ourselves when life gets hectic. Learning to respond to events from a place of calm and not being reactive by rather proactive and choosing thoughtfully. If there is only one take away from your journey with me I hope it is to incorporate meditation into your child's everyday life.

Conclusion

Guiding our children isn't about forcing them to do what we want, it is about guiding these beams of light and giving them space and freedom to live their lives as who they are meant to be lived.

I hope that everyone has enjoyed this journey with me and learned something useful along the way. Parenting with our whole hearts and being mindful is a practice that must be cultivated every day. Just like brushing our teeth eventually becomes a habit the more we do it, so will connecting with our full presence. When our children are guided from a place of wholeness and total acceptance of who they are and were sent here to be the world becomes filled with beautiful souls who change the world for the better.

Some of us spend our entire adult lives, healing from the first 18 years of our adolescence and it doesn't have to be that way. When we parent from a conscious place with an open heart we allow our children to freely step into their authentic selves.

Encouraging Books
(as my son has named them) and Resources

The Little Soul and the Earth by Neale Donald Walsh. This book gives children insight into their life before they came to Earth.

Have You Filled a Bucket Today? A Guide for Daily Happiness for Kids by Carol McCloud. It teaches children to think about how their actions and the actions of others affect us and how we can fill someone else's bucket by doing nice things for them.

Grasper by Paul Owen Lewis. A little crab learns that in order to grow a big heart you must keep a soft and heart and not be afraid to explore shores unknown.

I Knew You Could!: A Book for All the Stops in Your Life By Craig Dorfman and Cristina Ong. A new take on the classic *I Think I Can* using the train as a metaphor for a child's journey through life, this book is useful for children of all ages.

I believe in you By Marianne Richmond

Unstoppable Me By Dr. Wayne W. Dyer with Kristina Tracy

A Course in Miracles

To learn more about your child's learning style visit *http://vark-learn.com/*

Printed in the United States
By Bookmasters